OREGON
Concealed

OREGON Concealed

A Concealment Primer

Don W. Leach, Doctor of Laws

The Oregonconcealed.com Edition

Printed in the United States, the State of Oregon

ISBN: 978-0-9818062-0-4

Cover Design: by Don Leach

Book design by: Maureen Cutajar
www.gopublished.com

Attention: Instructors, clubs, organizations, and interested parties; please contact
www.oregonconcealed.com for quantity discounts or call our administrator
"Linda" @ 541-908-6548

Contents

Introduction

The moment you decide to exercise your federal Second Amendment right, or your Oregon Article 1, Section 27 right to carry a concealed handgun—legally or not—you need to know state laws. The purpose of *Oregon Concealed* is to help concealed handgun carriers understand both their responsibilities as well as Oregon law with real world application of the when, where, and how of lawful concealed handgun carry and use. *Oregon Concealed* is not meant to be a general discussion of the merits and/or shortcomings of Oregon's gun laws. Instead, the reader will precisely understand the outcomes and applications of the law resulting from an individual's choice to carry a concealed handgun.

Real World Examples for Understanding Contemporary Laws

Oregon Concealed is organized into chapters that make for easy to find substantive views on different aspects or applications of the law, and current issues surrounding those applications. Many currently available books on this subject deal mainly with federal Second Amendment issues and consist of broad debates about gun laws. Some reiterate Oregon laws, but fail to cover the nuances and dilemma of choices confronting those who choose to carry a handgun. *Oregon Concealed* presents, in clear and straightforward terms, what every gun owner who wishes to carry a concealed handgun must know. It is written in plain English.

Oregon Concealed does not pretend to be apolitical. Ending chapters give the author's political perspective, but only as it pertains to understanding the layered gun laws as they are applied today. The views stated are the author's, but they are offered to the reader as context in which to understand Oregon gun laws as a whole, for the purpose of helping you, the handgun owner and carrier, understand what is necessary to lawfully carry a concealed handgun.

Areas of Evolving / Devolving Law for Balance and Understanding

The examples in *Oregon Concealed* are true, taken from my case files as a practicing attorney. However, most of the names and locations have been changed to protect privacy; e.g. John Smith, Jane Smith, Bad Guy 1 or 2, etc. from Somewhere, Pandora County. Police, whether State, County, or City are referred to as Officer 1, 2, etc.

As the author my goal is to give you a complete understanding on the application of the concealed gun laws in Oregon in order that you may make informed decisions. The choice to carry concealed lawfully is the reader's, but I believe that responsible gun owners can and should follow the law as it is applied today if they want to keep their involvement with enforcement minimal.

CHAPTER 1

Concealed

Proceeding with a couple of fundamentals, let's insure we are all building our understanding of the parameters surrounding the lawful carrying of a concealed handgun in Oregon. The common law for Oregon was compiled in the first book of *General Laws for Oregon* – 1843 to 1872 by Deady and Lane.

The laws of Oregon in this book are like the book, antiques. Whether one goes to www.abebooks.com or some other source, we find the book generally available from $850 to $2,500, depending on its condition. Except for their historical value, these laws are for the most part valueless, having been changed by the legislated codified system we call "statutes."

Within the approximately 923 pages of this book are all the laws of Oregon from territorial governance to 1872. There are no laws concerning the carrying of concealed handguns, nor is there a definition of what a concealed handgun is. We leap forward from 1872 to the present and search the Oregon Revised Statutes and Administrative Rules. Again, we find no definitions for the term "concealed handgun."

We turn to the web (the Internet, not Webster) for dictionaries and information about the term of legal art, "concealed handgun." We learn there is no federal law specifically addressing the issuance of concealed handgun carry permits or licenses or even what "concealed" means with respect to handguns.[1] We also learn this matter of definition rests in the several states for their own interpretation (a States' Rights application).

In Oregon, historically there have been issues between the District, Circuit, Court of Appeal, and the Supreme Court concerning statutory construction and analysis. In 1978 the Oregon Supreme Court, in a rare moment of clarity, brought a unifying understanding on how the laws of Oregon were to be interpreted. That case, simply called *PGE*[2] by attorneys, judges, and the Oregon legislature set a standard that has been adopted in many of the states.

PGE is potentially much more complex than presented here,[3] but at the core the Oregon Supreme Court says that to understand what the statute means we first start with the plain meaning of words in the statute. After the next quick trip into "statute land" we will together do just that, interpret statutes in a simple and easy way to understand them.

All of the statutes are to be written so that a person with a reasonable education can understand what they and administrative laws say on their face. See the Oregon Constitution Article IV, Section 21.[4] The statutes,[5] just as the administrative rules, are to be written in a straightforward understandable format.[6] Remember, even though administrative laws are not written, or even functionally reviewed by the "law makers," which by operation of our Constitution is limited solely in the Legislative Branch, those administrative rules written by the Executive Branch still have the force and effect of statutes as if they had been written by the Legislative Branch and passed into law by the law making process. But I digress.

The "crime" of carrying a concealed firearm without a license is a Class A Misdemeanor with criminal liabilities and sanctions. Such a charge can lead to jail time and a fine. It becomes a part of the offender's criminal record and will follow him or her for years. Of course the district attorney has the latitude to treat such a crime as a "violation" which means that it is NOT a crime. Instead the charge will be reduced to merely a fine and will NOT create, or be on, a criminal record. Our web site, www.oregonconcealedlaw.com lists the current statutory laws applicable to concealed handguns.

It is important to understand the "concealed" concept. With the background we have provided above, with no statutory or administrative law definitions of the word "concealed" in the law, it becomes a term of legal art with its common meaning. Flowing from this treatment and attached to the statute is a "mens re" or "criminal mind set." The alleged "criminal" had to have intended to conceal, to hide, or to secret his gun on his or her person, or within his or her control to be guilty of the crime of wrongfully carrying a concealed handgun.

- To carry concealed, one has to intend the handgun be hidden from view and/or secreted so that others cannot see it.

John Smith's Pickup Ride

John Smith was driving down a back county highway in the county of Pandora. The 1965 beat-up, mostly green and rust Chevy farm pick-up had some new interior with black leather bucket seats that had replaced the old bench seat. When he was stopped by County Officer 1 ("CO1"), the officer informed John his left tail light was out. The usual questions followed with John's presentation of the required documentation, license, and registration. During the stop Mr. Smith indicated his surprise to find the tail light was out, and asked if he could get out and see it, "After all it is my son's rig. He has done so much work on it to make it street legal so of course I am surprised."

"Of course," was the officer's reply. As the police would say, Mr. Smith "exited the vehicle." As John slid across the lipped edge of the bucket seat and turned to walk back to the driver side tail light he left the door open.

It was the officer's turn to be surprised. "John, is that your gun?" There, in what was now plain view, stuck between the bucket seats with the handle showing was what turned out to be a Smith & Wesson long barrel .357 magnum.

"Yea, that is my gun."

The officer, doing what enforcement does asked, "Why did you conceal it between the seats?"

John probably looked sorry, "It was sliding around and I didn't want it to fall on the floorboard."

The nature of the officer's question was to elicit a response where the now suspect Mr. Smith would admit his wrong doing. The answer to the question infers an admission on the part of Mr. Smith that he was in fact carrying a concealed firearm.

"John, do you have a license to carry that gun concealed?"

This is another question requesting inferentially the admission to a crime. John's short "No" was enough. Even though Officer 1 and Mr. Smith had been neighbors some time, the officer became all business.

"Sorry John. I am going to have to arrest you." And he did. He offered to call a family member to retrieve the pickup (which was outside of protocol). John accepted.

When this case came to me for representation of John, I thought this was a matter that would be dropped by the Assistant DA, or reduced to a violation with a warning to Mr. Smith. In my naivety I thought the system would get a pound of money instead of flesh while sending the message to the community not to carry concealed handguns without a license. But whether due to her newness, direction from the DA, or for whatever reason, we found ourselves in trial in the small town of Somewhere in rural Oregon. My client was offered an opportunity to waive the jury, but insisted on his constitutional right to have one in a criminal trial. In the due course of time we went to trial with a six-person jury.

We presented the facts as you have read them above. Mr. Smith testified that he had put the gun between the seats to keep it from sliding out of the buck seat on the passenger side. He noted he had been "up in the mountains where the roads were rough." He added that he had no intention to "conceal" the revolver. He told the jury it could easily be seen from the other side of the pickup. He testified to the fact that the butt of the gun was pointing toward the front of the pickup. He asked them if a "criminal" would have done that. He denied with passion that he admitted he was carrying concealed.

The DA recalled Officer 1. She asked him, "Was the butt of the gun pointed toward the front of the vehicle?"

"Yes."

Verdict: Not guilty.

Of course, this happening has a number of pearls of wisdom in it. In a traffic stop the trial starts with the first question from the officer's mouth. Second, the questions are designed to elicit "admissions." That means exactly what the word says. From this example we learn an important point: admit nothing during the stop that can be used against us.

In law school, by the time we had our degree and were ready to take the bar exam for Oregon, we had law school down to its simplest forms. Year 1; Admit nothing. Year 2; Deny everything. Year 3; Counter charge.

If an officer stops me and asks something like, "Did you know you were speeding?"

"Absolutely not and I don't know it now."

"I have you on radar at 122 mph." That officer's statement does not call for a response so I would not make one.

They ask, "Would you like to see the radar?"

In my case I would respond, "Absolutely not."

And so it goes.

- To unlawfully carry concealed one has to have the mental state or "mens re" to commit a crime.
- The "stop" starts when the blue and red lights come on.
- The "trial" starts when the blue and red lights come on.
- The enforcement officer looks for admissions.
- If you feel compelled to speak, admit nothing.
- Deny everything.
- Counter charge.

John & Jane Smith's Fight

John and Jane Smith were traveling on the I-5 corridor in the county of Pandora on their way to the city of Somewhere. The Smith's fun and lofty goal as they started their late September journey was to visit one of their sons and his family, the grandchildren. It was hot outside, and perhaps that is a strong understatement of the weather condition. We could say it was "hot" inside too, but a different kind of hot.

As some married folks do, they were verbally fighting. The subject matter bounced from the long drive ahead of them to the weather, a lack of money, and such other things married and other folks fight about. John's anger was escalating. Of course in working so hard to be heard he did not notice he had increased his speed significantly while shouting at his wife. Nor did he immediately notice the flashing lights. The agreed facts were that John had no idea Officer 1 was behind him until he heard the siren. John did not know how far he had traveled and relied on Officer 1's statement it was over a mile.

Being of a persuasion that one should not be stopped for the purposes of taxing when there is no issue surrounding the concept of a "victim," his anger was escalated. For those who do not know, this is generally considered a somewhat radical right wing concept: Before there can be a crime there has to be a victim and that victim has to be a real person.

Officer 1 ran the license plate, finding Mr. Smith had an Oregon Concealed Handgun License issued to him. It was with caution the officer approached the newer SUV. Mr. Smith had his hands on the steering wheel at the 11:00 position just as recommended by the NRA in their safety program for Basic Pistol Training.

"Are you John Smith?" As trained, the officer was standing by the driver's door, but a little back, turned a little sideways, with one hand on the butt of his holstered pistol.

Looking straight ahead, the one-word response was short and filled with anger, "Yes!"

"Do you have a concealed handgun license and if so, are you carrying?"

Mr. Smith's answer was even more harsh-sounding. "I don't have to tell you, shit head."

The officer drew his gun, pointing it at the ground but at the ready. "Get out of the car." The rest of the initial stop was like many seen on television, with Mr. Smith leaning palms down on the hood of the SUV, its metal already almost too hot to touch. Mrs. Smith remained seated, with the appearance of being calm, hands folded in her lap.

The officer asked Mrs. Smith if there was a gun and if there was where it was.

Mr. Smith spoke up, "You don't have to tell him. Don't tell him."

She looked at the officer, then pointed with her right hand at the console. "In there officer."

"Please sit there and do not move," he asked her.

The officer's conversation with dispatch was short, the call for backup barely audible to Mr. and Mrs. Smith.

"Whatcha doing that for?" Mr. Smith sounded just as belligerent as when he was first stopped.

It did not take long before the county sheriff "backup" deputy arrived on the scene.

The handgun, a 9mm Glock 17 was loaded (more on that later). Before the stop was complete Mr. Smith was cited for excessive speed, and Mrs. Smith who was without a concealed handgun license for Oregon was arrested for two misdemeanor counts. The first was for unlawful possession of a concealed handgun. The second count was for the unlawful possession of a loaded concealed handgun in a vehicle upon the highways and byways of Oregon.

Oregon applies an "accessibility" standard by statute, which in substance declares a handgun in the traveling compartment is "accessible" to all in the vehicle. While the statute is direct and clear, it is generally treated as a presumption that can be overcome factually. For example, is the handgun actually accessible if one does not know it is there? An alternative question is whether the handgun is truly accessible if it is physically being carried by the other person and cannot be accessed? Yet a third question deals with whether the handgun can be accessed in a glove box or console.

While this story is a long one from here, the main thrust was that through my conversations I convinced the DA of Pandora County to treat the matter as a violation. As a part of the deal, he insisted on, and my clients agreed, to give up the Glock 17 in addition to the fine.

I tell my concealed classes that I have represented clients in a number of ORS 166.250(1) cases (unlawful carry of a concealed firearm) and never lost one. I was lucky on this one in that the DA agreed to be reasonable. I think that otherwise if this case had gone to a jury, there was a real possibility I would have had at least one client with a criminal finding of "guilty" for a concealed handgun crime.

The leverage on the DA for the reduction to "violation" treatment was that the officer used the wife to beat up the husband because of the husband's poor attitude and offensive demeanor. That would make her jury friendly. It helped that she was from a generational "old family–old money" in Pandora County with lots of timber money behind them, and known to donate substantially to the particular political party the DA belonged to. The promise of a large audience to hear how the officer took out his frustration on the wife who was calmly sitting there certainly weighed in the decision-making process. After all, no one likes a wife beater, and she wasn't even the officer's wife.

Again, there are pearls of wisdom gleaned from this case. The stop, if otherwise amicable, can certainly be driven to a different place by the actions of the object of the stop. The NRA recommendations come from a long historical perspective based on tested best practices. The NRA suggests a person being stopped puts his or her hands at the 11:00. If the object of the stop wants to be belligerent and abusive, to demand their constitutional rights, we suggest he or she wait until a better time to insist on such rights. As a practical matter might the situation and the person being stopped might be better served in following the Zen counsel, all things in moderation. It certainly is considered in good form as well.

- It is recommended both by the NRA and by Oregon Concealed for the purposes of a stop, the driver puts his or her hands at the 11:00 o'clock position on the steering wheel.
- If the licensed person in the vehicle is carrying a concealed handgun, it should not be accessible to an unlicensed person in the vehicle.
- It is our recommendation the licensed person carrying concealed keeps it concealed, which includes not sharing information about having a handgun or where it is located with passengers.
- Oregon has an "accessibility" statute which carries the presumption a handgun in a vehicle is available to those in the vehicle. We recommend the licensed person keeps the handgun on their person,
- or in a place where the passengers cannot get to it
- and the passengers are not told about it.

Testing for Gold

John Smith and Close Friend had a gold claim on Water Creek. They brought ore samples to Mr. Friend's house to conduct some preliminary flame testing for gold and other minerals. Mr. Friend's house was in the town of Somewhere, immediately behind the local Post Office. Mr. Friend carried home the Marlin 30–30 he always had with him when he went to his gold claim with his partner Mr. Smith. He put the 30–30 on the back porch near where the oxyacetylene tanks were.

Mr. Smith and Mr. Friend were dressed in the work clothes of miners, with heavy steel-toed boots, faded and torn blue jeans, and plaid shirts. Both had western-styled cowboy straw hats on this particular hot summer day. Mr. Smith's hat was pulled low over his eyes. Of course they wore hard hats when exploring old mining site slopes and portals and when they were working their claim. But they had changed hats when they left the mine site. Both had dirty, scraggly beards. Mr. Smith had dark glasses he was wearing for the flame tests while Mr. Friend used the goggles designed for eye protection from the brightness of the flame.

A leather vest hung well over Mr. Smith's tall, slender frame. Under the vest was a .357 Magnum Long Barreled Smith & Wesson carried vertically in a shoulder holster on the left side, the bulge almost invisible. Mr. Smith favored the shoulder holster because as he said later, "I can keep my hands free to use the mining tools, and the tools designed for self-preservation."

Unknown to Smith and Friend, another citizen neighbor had called 911 reporting strange activity behind the Post Office, men with beards and guns. It was of course reported that both were armed, one with a pistol, the other with a rifle. The 911 dispatcher sent the city police.

Officer 1, a large man of about 5'10" and 265 pounds approached Smith and Friend from the north. Officer 2 approached from the south, both stopping at the property lot line which was fenced with the gate closed. "Can we speak to you?" The officers had to ask louder the second time to be heard over the sound of the torch. Misters Smith and Friend removed their eye protection, turning to face the officers.

Mr. Smith asked, "Can we help you officers?"

Officer 1 who had approached the property from the north, Mr.

Smith's left, said, "We have some questions for you."

Mr. Smith asked, "Do you have a warrant?"

Officer 2 responded, "No."

Mr. Smith looked down his nose. "Get one." He turned back to the testing, still having the burning torch in his hand. Friend lowered his own goggles back over his eyes, also returning to the flame test.

Officer 1 pulled his gun, pointing it at Mr. Smith, and shouting said, "You are under arrest. You are under arrest. Get down on the ground and spread them. You know the drill." Pointing with his pistol toward the ground, he shouted again, "Get down on the ground!"

From this incident Mr. Smith was originally arrested for carrying a concealed handgun. He was frisked by both officers before getting into the police car handcuffed. At the police station he was searched again before going into the station. The jailer searched Mr. Smith yet again. They took his vest, boots, and belt. They already had the gun, holster, knife, and sheath. During the booking, while Mr. Smith was enjoying the intake process in yet another area of the jail, Officer 1 found a hashish pipe in the liner of Mr. Smith's vest, or so he claimed. A misdemeanor drug paraphernalia charge was added to the list of concealed handgun crimes.

I was and am a friend of the family. So when time came to make the call, Mr. Smith called me.

Things progressed in the normal fashion of such charges. At the appropriate time I made a motion to have the drug charged dismissed. The grounds for the dismissal was that no jury could make any finding of guilty considering the fact that Officer 1 "planted" the evidence. The judge granted my motion without making a finding that Officer 1 planted the evidence, warning Officer 1 that he, the Judge, would not tolerate abuse of the process.

At the trial I asked the officer witnesses be kept from the room. This included the arresting officer, his partner, and the jailer.

The trial was interesting. Officer 2 testified that as he walked up to the fence, he saw the butt of the revolver and part of the shoulder holster. He further testified they were in the yard of Mr. Friend, behind a closed gate, and that there was a "No Trespassing" sign on the gate.

Mr. Friend testified he could see the gun at all times. Both Officers 1 and 2 testified they arrived at the scene as the result of being directed by dispatch, noting dispatch told them both Mr. Smith and Friend had guns. Officer 1 testified that he could not see the handgun at all and therefore it was concealed.

Q: How long have you known Mr. Smith?

A: Since grade school.

Q: You went to high school together?

A: Yes.

Q: Were you best friends?

A: No.

Q: Did you get into a fight in high school?

A: (Reluctantly) Yes.

Q: Would it be fair to say Mr. Smith beat you soundly, in front of many of your friends?

(Looking sullen he refused to answer. I went on.) I have your high school sweet heart here. She can testify to this if you prefer.

A: Yea, I lost the fight.

Q: And didn't you promise to get even if it took the rest of your life?

A: I guess so.

Q: So isn't the truth of this matter you saw this as your opportunity to do just that, get even?

A: (No answer.)

I asked the judge for an opportunity for a demonstration. The court granted it. I asked Officer 1 if he would put on the belt with the knife and the holster with gun in it, as it was when he saw it on Mr. Smith. I suggested that after all we want to keep the gun out of the hands of such a dangerous person as Mr. Smith, so he, the officer, was the more appropriate person.

The assistant DA objected to my comment, and the judge warned me outside the presence of the jury; and then after the jury came back and were seated the judge ordered the jury to disregard my comment noting that it had no evidentiary value.

Most enforcement officers are good people trying hard to do their job the best they can. In an environment of underfunding, high political pressures, and reduced staffing, sometimes it is amazing they can get done what they do. In this instance I was dealing with the other type of cop, one who sees his job as his baby. It ain't ugly and he will lie to prove it. This case also had an overlay of revenge.

We return to the trial and the demonstration. Officer 1 without other prompting tried to put on the belt. It was too small for him so he put it back down on the assistant district attorney's table. He put on the shoulder holster. It was adjusted too small for his large body frame but he did get it on.

I sat there amazed the DA let me go through the exercise without any objections.

Officer 1 asked if I wanted him to put the gun in the holster. Of course I said "yes." Then, "Please put the vest on." He did and it didn't fit either. Worse for him, with the butt of the holstered handgun jutting forward, the vest did not reach far enough to fully cover the holster or gun, so the view from any angle showed the gun. He fumbled trying to make it right from his perspective. One of the jury members actually snickered.

Q: So, Officer 1, what does concealed mean?

A: Ahh, ahh, it means to have it where the police cannot see it.

DA: Objection. Officer 1 is not an attorney.

We proceeded to discuss this outside the presence of the jury after they were sent to the jury room, again. My part of the discussion centered on the foundation questions where it was established Officer 1 knew the law and it was his job to enforce it. He made the arrest so he had to know the elements of the "crime." Also argued was that concealment was a cornerstone of the offense and Officer 1 had to understand what "concealed" means to arrest Mr. Smith on that charge.

The DA continued his same song. "Officer 1 is not an attorney and therefore could not know the law." The DA's argument was as ludicrous as Officer 1 trying to fit that holster and vest onto his fat body.

The judge's findings were that as an enforcement officer of the Executive Branch of government, Officer 1 had to know the law well enough to enforce it. And that meant, at a minimum, as the arresting officer he had to know what "concealed" meant. The judge denied the motion and after the jury was again seated denied the motion for the record in the jury's presence. He asked me to proceed.

Q: Is it true that to "conceal" means one secrets or hides the gun on purpose?

A: I guess so.

Q: Do you really think the gun was hidden?

A: Yes.

Q: On purpose?

A: Yes.

Q: Even though Mr. Friend, Officer 2, and even you could see it?

A: Yes.

In preparation for the trial I had created what is called a *trial brief* for the judge, outlining the issues as I saw them and the testimony I expected to receive. That document included an outline of the law surrounding what is and is not "concealed."

After both sides had "rested" their case the judge sent the jury back to the jury room without instructions. Then he asked me if I wanted to make a motion for a finding based on the evidence that no responsible jury could possibly make a finding of "guilty" on the evidence submitted.

I was somewhat dumbfounded. At that time I was new enough to the practice of law I didn't know I could do that. Of course I said "yes." He then asked the DA if he wanted to argue further. The DA just shook his head in the negative.

The judge looked down his nose a little from the bench. "Call everybody back in." The clerk did so whereupon the judge dismissed the jury. Then he outlined the motion I was surprised I made. He said he had a few comments "before I grant the motion."

The judge looked at the DA then at Officer 1. "Of course you know we judges talk. We meet once a week and I will be discussing this case and your handling of it." He was looking directly at Officer 1. "It is the order of this court that you, Officer 1, do not appear in my court again until the DA's or sheriff's office has given me documentation showing you have completed 40 hours of course material in ethical conduct by public employees. The motion of the defendant's counsel is granted. Case dismissed."

- For a handgun to be concealed there has to be an "intent" to conceal.

Deer Hunting

When John Smith started trekking toward his deer stand with the GPS in hand and following the way-points, it was well before day light. The air was blustery, almost warm, with no hint of how bad it was going to get. But it would not have mattered to Mr. Smith because on this day in the outback of Pandora County, with his 18-day-old, but otherwise brand new, 30-06 Winchester rifle, it was the last day of the season. The moss-backed deer he had watched off and on through the summer, one of the biggest white-tailed bucks he had ever seen, had found a good hiding place and somehow managed to elude the persistent hunter.

John found the stand with no difficulty, at about 15 minutes before shooting light. Crouched and ready, he waited. Even though arguable it was not yet shooting light, he scoped the trail, thinking unconsciously that with the big 12X Weaver, he could shoot if he had the opportunity because the scope drew in enough light for reasonable visibility. With that thought behind him while slowly swinging the rifle following the trail along the side hill of the draw he spotted the old deer.

It had been a lot of years since he had buck fever so he didn't even feel it coming on. As he was trying to align the scope with the deer the gun went off before he was ready, "KaPow!" The crack of the bullet breaking the sound barrier as it headed down range was sickening to John because he knew he had shot too high, over the back of an aged Bambi. Frantic in working the bolt action he did not have time to get the rifle re-aligned for a second shot, for the deer had already disappeared.

Knowing if he were to have another opportunity he would have to track the buck down, John went down the hill to the trail where he had last seen the buck. Sure enough, there were the fresh tracks. Leaning down John put his fingers in the dew claw marks. He stood, shaking his head slowly from side to side. The deer had to be one of the biggest he had ever seen.

During the next three to four hours the weather kept getting worse, with the "worse" compounding. It was hard work staying on top of the track, keeping it visible, and following it. John jumped the buck twice more but in each situation he did not have time to shoot before the deer again disappeared. The last time it was the rolling dark gray fog that started overlaying the ground the buck turned into, disappearing as if it were a ghost.

The one thing John wanted, that he gave a deer hunter's prayer for, was there would be no rain. To his dismay the drizzle started, not enough to call rain yet. Without conscious thought he automatically buttoned his Carhartt® long waistcoat to protect himself, and the otherwise openly carried revolver on his right hip.

Just topping the next hill in the middle of outback at nowhere in Pandora county, another opportunity presented itself as the big buck thinking it was sneaking with its head down in the fog turned, following a small brush line crossing the clearing John had just slipped into. John with deliberation this time took careful aim. The second "Ka-pow" of the day echoed across the hill sides. The elation that filled John was punched out of him with these words coming from his right, "Nice shot!"

John had not heard nor seen the man until he spoke. It was an Oregon State Trooper dressed in the greens they sometimes wear when they are engaged in enforcing the hunting laws of Oregon while in the wild. John could not help but look to see if "Murphy" was the name on the officer's name tag. But it was Officer 1, not the infamous Murphy known in this area for his enforcement abilities and hard attitudes.

The officer, walking toward John from about only 20 feet away asked, "Got your hunting license, tag, I.D.?"

John still in a state of surprise and the additional adrenaline flowing from the shock said, "Yes, got it all right here," patting his right hip pocket through the jacket.

The officer walked up to him, "Then let's make this quick. You will want to get that buck taken care of right away. Gonna rain." Both looked up at the blackening clouds through the fog and sprinkle already starting to get things wet as it was now falling more steadily.

John unbuttoned his jacket reaching for his wallet when the officer saw the holstered handgun.

Uncharacteristic of state police officers and probably in violation of protocol, after making the arrest for unlawfully carrying concealed but before handcuffing John, they went down to the deer and prepped it to carry it out. Some of John's family recovered the buck later that day.

This situation could have taken a lot of different directions, a citation for a violation as opposed to an arrest for the misdemeanor of carrying a concealed handgun. The DA could have reduced or dropped the charges. And so on. But almost five months later we were headed to trial.

The officer provided no testimony to the "intent" of Mr. Smith. He presented the facts of his observations well, and they were consistent with those John presented. His statement that the gun being concealed stood alone. Cross-examination showed other than the officer's inability to see the handgun there was no other evidence of "concealment." The officer admitted to the conditions of the weather and that it was likely Mr. Smith had "covered" his handgun just as he claimed. Before I could stop him Officer 1 added, "but it was concealed because I couldn't see it."

So I inquired further:

Q: What does concealed mean?

A: That I couldn't see it.

Q: But really, what does concealed mean?

A: That the gun in this case was hidden from view.

Q: Are you saying that you merely couldn't see it or are you saying Mr. Smith deliberately hid his gun from you.

A: Well, no. I think he covered it just as he told me he did, but in doing that he hid it from me and the rest of the world. So it was concealed.

I did not inquire further.

The DA tried to resurrect the case, but did nothing in his redirect examination to help his witness. I did not try to re-cross-examine Officer 1.

At this later date being more mature in the law, I made the appropriate motion to dismiss for lack of evidence showing the intent or "mens-re" on the part of the defendant, that the uncontroverted facts in this case showed the handgun was merely covered, not concealed. I offered that no jury could on the basis of the evidence find Mr. Smith guilty.

This judge was not as understanding of the law, or else he was anti-gun. He ruled against my motion even though my trial brief fully outlined the actual testimony given and the applicable law, the same law as from the earlier case. Fortunately, the jury did understand the law. Mr. Smith was found "Not guilty."

Summary

These are actual cases reinforcing the concept that one has to have the intent to break the concealed handgun law before they can be guilty of the criminal act. They also show other views of how the law is to be interpreted. The mere lack of visibility does not mean the handgun is concealed. Also, there are a number of reasons why a gun may not be visible that are viable "excuses" for having it in a condition where it cannot be seen. Go to www.oregonconcealed.com – Review ORS 161.085(2), (5) through (9).

More important to the reader who is going to take away knowledge of experiences related in this chapter is the fact that responsibility and prudence dictate certain appropriate actions if one wishes to avoid conflict issues. This, we believe, is the start of wisdom in the responsible acts of carrying a handgun concealed within the meanings of the law.

We also believe this prudence economically protects the wary from the taxing authorities who use the criminal code to raise revenue, and attorneys who use the civil and criminal code to merely make a living. We remind you of the Coburg police who were stopping speeders on the freeway to raise revenue for their city just north of Eugene, Oregon.

CHAPTER 2

Deadly Force

The Standard for Use of Deadly Force

A person is authorized by statute to use deadly physical force in defense of self or third parties in their presence where the person using deadly force is using it to protect him or herself or the third party from the wrongful (felony) use of deadly force or other force likely to produce death or serious bodily injury by the Bad Guy (BG). The defensive force being used for protection can only be used for as long as is necessary to eliminate the wrongful use or imminent use of felony (deadly) force or other unlawful physical force likely to produce death or serious bodily injury.[7]

Over the years I have been asked many times in class whether it is OK to make sure the Bad Guy is dead. Should the shooter drag BG in the house, and other such questions. We do not and will not venture upon this slippery ground. The answer is not one of whether the statute is a license to kill. It is not.[8] So if Bad Guy has been incapacitated or no longer has the means to engage the imminent use of unlawful physical force, then the statutory authorization to use a deadly force response is terminated.

There are other boundaries. We advise our classes to watch out for mutual combatant situations. You cannot agree to fight and then use that fight to justify a deadly force response.[9] The decision to use a deadly force response must be based on a *reasonable belief* the forceful response and the amount of the forceful response used was necessary to eliminate the threat under the standard. In the court system this reasonable belief will be tested by a reasonable and prudent person standard as it is applied here in Oregon.

This means in the event there are criminal charges or a civil action flowing from the incident, a jury or a judge if the jury is waived, will make the decision concerning whether the responsive force used was reasonable. They will ask and answer this question in some form, "If a reasonably prudent person were in a similar factual situation and they made the decision to use deadly force in that circumstance, would that deadly force response be justified?"

So you or the person caught in the circumstances has to make a potentially life and death decision in often a mere fraction of a second. For your action, the totality of the circumstances surrounding your belief will be taken into consideration. Was your reasonable belief necessary to guard against the use or imminent use of unlawful physical force? Was the degree of force you used based on a subjective belief and if the decision is "yes," then was it was necessary? Knowing the inquiry standard is the prudent person standard, it follows that the belief which was reasonable to you under the immediacy of your circumstances may not be enough by itself where the arbitrators have minutes, hours, even days to determine whether your belief was reasonable.

The Catch-22 in this process is that it is possible through our system, in our honest belief and assessment of the circumstances, under the then conditions in which we found ourselves, which when reviewed may not be enough to justify the use of a deadly force. The bottom line is our belief has to be objective enough, as judged by the jury or judge they would arrive at the same conclusion we did under those circumstances.[10]

The nature of the use of deadly force we are talking about here is some form of the use of self-defense for ourselves and/or for the benefit of others in our presence.

Judged by 12 or Carried by 6?

Mrs. Jane Smith had several strokes over the last three years. In fact, the seven identified were cumulative enough that she was bed-ridden in her home. Her condition was considered "fragile." The personal care she received, while not every minute of the day, was 24/7 and mostly provided by her husband John. She was 67 and he was 65, married since they were in their early 20s. They had been high school sweethearts.

Mr. Smith's work was through his business of over 40 years, in his shop right next to the highway. He made *Thingys*. They fit on interstate trucks making the tedious hours of driving more bearable and safer. He had three employees. John also worked long hours but that was OK. For the benefit of his wife John had hooked up a baby monitor he kindly called "an emergency adult communication device." All his life it seemed he had called Jane "Baby" so this too was OK with her as well.

Perhaps due to the conditions in which he lived, Mr. Smith emphasized the need for all of us to exercise our actions in such a way as to allow others to have their dignity recognized and honored. Based on that belief, John provided honor and gave recognition to the desires of his wife, to provide her all of the quality and dignity possible under the trying circumstances they found themselves.

Being not only an entrepreneur but also an inventor, John had designed and wired in a flashing light so that when the monitor went off, not only would there be the sounds of communication, but a visual to draw his attention to the adult communication device in the event he could not hear it. Their manufactured home was only about two hundred feet from the business shop next to the highway so the arrangement worked well.

Sometime in the early 1990s John had gone to bed after their prayers, cuddled with his wife, accepting of what was and of course wishing as always things might be a little better on the morrow for his sweetheart of so many years. It had been a long day and a struggle for each of them in their own way. It was going to be a restless night, and like so many before they would get through it.

Sometime after one o'clock in the morning Bad Guy and Weasel, who was riding the "bitch" seat of the Harley Davidson Pan Head motorcycle, ran out of gas. As misfortune would have it, the bike stopped right in front of John's *Thingy* Business. Bad Guy and Weasel (W) decided to look for a hose so they could siphon some gas for the bike from one of the trucks at the shop.

The noise of their rummaging woke John who was not sleeping well. He got up and looked through the window in the direction of the noise, under the flood lights at the business. There was also a flood light near his home so the general area was well lit considering the hour. It was almost 1:30 in the morning. He saw two men he did not recognize. John looked at the clock on the bed stand, then at the bedroom phone. He dialed 911.

John explained the problem, gave the 911 operator the address of the business and asked for instructions.

"Stay in the house," she said, adding, "I have dispatched the Sheriff's deputies. They should be their momentarily." As they both hung up, he looked at the clock again. Less than two minutes had passed on the call. It was now 1:34 a.m. As the bad guys moved further back from the front of Mr. Smith's business manufacturing building toward his home in their search, time passed.

At 1:45 a.m. John called again. "This is John Smith, I called earlier..."

Dispatch: I know who you are.

John: Yes. They are getting closer to my house.

Dispatch: I have alerted the deputies, they are on the way.

John: I am sure of that, but worried, my wife...

He did not get to finish his statement before she interrupted:

Dispatch: I told you they are on their way.

She hung up.

When John called back again at 1:52 a.m. the same dispatcher's comments were short, clipped, and rude, with her ending by telling him the deputies would get there whenever they got there, but that they were on their way. Then she again hung up.

John called again at 1:57 a.m., 24 minutes after his first call. The same dispatch lady was again ignorant to him, only this time her rudeness went beyond the normal bounds of societal acceptance, a rant such that if she had been anyone else's employee that I know, she would have been fired. She ended her tirade with, "I told you they are on their way."

John in a quiet voice said, "Oh, you misunderstand this call. You don't need to send the deputies. I just shot one of them [the intruders] so I don't need a deputy." This time he hung up on her.

When I tell this story in the concealed classes I ask, "So how long did it take for the deputies to show up? There were 3 cars, 4 deputies, 1 State officer. How long?" The guesses usually range from 3 minutes to as long as another 35 minutes.

The true answer is 38 seconds!

In answer to the next question of where were they: John's business on the highway was separated from an all-night doughnut shop by a small hill. As we prepared for trial later, we found the deputies had been there at the donut shop for their "break" the whole time.

BG had been wounded but not seriously. He had been shot through his hand taking BG's thumb off.

When the police arrived John told his story. When BG and W got near the house and started walking around his personal vehicle, John grabbed the rifle by the door and went out to confront them. John's concern was that if his wife had another seizure or bad moment he needed the car to be ready to go so he could take her to the hospital. BG messing around with it could cause serious repercussions in John's life if the car was needed but would not work. It could even be life threatening to his wife.

John said that when he ordered BG and W off the property, BG attacked him with something that looked like a knife. Bad Guy, as we were to learn later, was truly a real bad guy.

The sheriff's deputies took the position that John had used a gun so he was the real bad guy.

They took John to jail after giving him time to arrange for someone to come over and sit with his wife. John was booked for "Attempted Manslaughter – Felony III"

At almost 4:00 a.m. I got John's one phone call.

Backstory:

After graduating from law school and passing the bar I immediately set up a solo practice in 1989. John came to me on a False Arrest. He claimed he had been wrongly jailed for almost an hour. He was recommended to me through a mutual friend. For that false arrest we collected a few dollars, my portion being almost $40,000. From there I successfully represented him on several other issues so we had some positive history.

Continuing:

There is a lot more to this story not told in this short synopsis. A huge fight with the DA on what could and could not be evidence was engaged. Our investigator found the knife used to attack John lying in the field by the driveway where the confrontation happened. The blade was open. I add the deputies didn't even look for it. The knife had BG's fingerprints and blood on it. There was a copperized nick out of the handle, right next to where the now missing thumb would have been holding it.

We found, Bad Guy and Weasel had been on a four-day drug and sex binge, and were headed to another such party when they ran out of gas. And we found that BG had an almost unbelievable record of assault, attempted murder, etc. with no convictions. We found that witnesses in BG's past either refused to testify against him or in the alternative, went missing. Of course, I wanted all of that information to be presented at the trial.

Finally in a heart-to-heart with the DA in the hallway of the court-house, the DA was made to understand my client had money. All of the particulars of this abuse by his office would be written up, posted on every telephone pole in Pandora County, and sent to every registered voter. I suggested it would not bode well for him when the public learned that it was John's investigator who found the knife in the field where one would have expected to find it; with BG's blood on it; with BG's fingerprints on it; and copper traces imbedded in a nick on the handle of the knife. I suggested the fact the police didn't even look for the knife and his office continued with the prosecution of a man trying to defend his home and dying wife after learning of the knife, and I noted they hadn't even asked for verification of the truthfulness of our allegations. It was strongly suggested this would not bode well for his office. It was an election year.

The DA had a miraculous change of direction, two days later dropping all the charges. Another two working days later BG filed a civil lawsuit against John. It was months, before that ended in trial.

With $42,500 expenses in attorney and investigator fees John walked out of the courtroom for the last time (he prevailed in the civil suit). I asked John for the first time, "Why did you pick up the rifle instead of the pistol laying there?"

He shook his head a little, looked down on me (he was a tall man) and said, "Don, I just don't know. I have thought about it. I think that maybe being just a good old boy who has hunted all my life, I grabbed what I knew."

I was frustrated at the direction this had taken from the very first. "John, if you had just picked up the pistol. Maybe you would not have had to go through all of this. $42,500! And to go through the civil trial?"

"Yea yea. I know. I have thought a lot about this. But you know what?"

I shrugged trying in my mind to guess. I asked, "No. What?"

"Tried by 12 or carried by 6 has new meaning to me today! My only real regret has been what it cost my wife."

She had died shortly before the end of the civil trial.

It Wasn't for a Cup of Coffee

We spring forward from almost 20 years ago to an Oregon incident in the recent past.

November 24, 2010 at 9:00 p.m.: The focused attention to the facts obtained in the investigation of the Dutch Brothers shooting show two men approached the kiosk and at least one of them attempted to rob it. The barista—a 'coffee chef' to those who don't live in the heavily-caffeinated Pacific Northwest—throughout this incident and the aftermath was not publicly identified by authorities. Even though he shot and killed one of the men, and the investigation was homicide oriented, at all times the barista was treated as the "victim." It is the general policy of the police to honor the privacy of victims in these types of situations as well as in responsible reporting by the news media. Similarly, in this book, we obviously agree with that outlook on how a victim in these circumstances should be treated.

Early on, the Eugene police characterized the Dutch Brother's coffee-stand worker who fatally shot the would-be robber on that fateful Wednesday night as being the victim of a crime.[11] Even so, the detectives treated the incident on Franklin Boulevard just as they would any other homicide investigation. The barista told Eugene police he shot and killed the armed robber after the intruder momentarily looked away while holding him at gunpoint inside a Franklin Boulevard coffee kiosk. The barista pulled a Glock .40-caliber handgun from his waistband and fired several shots toward Sirus Combs, who collapsed and died in the coffee stand's doorway while clutching a wad of stolen cash in one hand and a pistol in the other.

The barista said Combs fired at least two gunshots toward him after he began shooting—the Dutch Brothers worker stepped outside the kiosk and encountered a second robber, who raised a handgun toward him. The barista fired twice toward Combs's accomplice, who returned fire and then ran from the scene. Later identified as the second person shot at, Plunk, 27, denied participating in the heist when Officer Braziel of the Eugene police interviewed him following his arrest according to an affidavit filed in the investigation.

The document details how, nearly two months after the robbery, police managed to track down Plunk at his Eugene home on a Friday. Officer Braziel wrote that he obtained key information in the case from a Lane County Jail inmate who helped police contact a witness to the crime.

The witness told Officer Braziel that on the night of the robbery, he used a stolen car to drive Combs and Plunk to a spot near the coffee stand and watched from across the street as the incident unfolded.

The witness "heard yelling and saw Combs was inside the Dutch Brothers building," Officer Braziel wrote. The man "heard six to eight gunshots, and saw Combs lying in the doorway ... [He] saw Plunk fire two gunshots from a handgun toward the building [and] saw Plunk run northeast bound toward the Willamette River. [The witness] wiped the stolen vehicle for fingerprints, and left the scene on foot."

The witness said Plunk told him a few hours later not to talk about the incident "because they were the only two who knew what happened, and that if they never talked then no one else would ever know."

Officer Braziel filed the affidavit document in Lane County Circuit Court to support criminal charges against Brandon Lee Plunk, as the man

who allegedly accompanied Combs to the coffee stand and exchanged gun-
fire with the barista before fleeing.

In the investigation process the police gathered as much evidence as
possible before presenting the case to Lane County prosecutors. They noted: "This is going to be handled like any other shooting. We want to make
sure that we're careful with [the investigation]." As stated above, the prosecutors ultimately determined the shooting was justified under Oregon law.

The general view of self-defense is that deadly force is legal in Oregon
only when used against a person who is reasonably believed to be committing a felony while using or threatening to use physical force that is intended to or can lead to death or serious bodily injury, or to defend against a
burglary in a dwelling.

Dutch Brothers company policy at the time of the incident prohibited
employees from carrying firearms at work.

The barista said in the affidavit that on the night of the robbery, he unlocked and opened the coffee stand's door for Combs after mistaking the
stranger for a co-worker.

Combs burst into the kiosk and pointed a handgun at the worker's
chest while threatening to kill him and demanding money. After the barista
allowed Combs to take cash from the till, Combs ordered him to turn
around. The worker "thought Combs was having him turn around so he
could execute him," Braziel wrote. As the barista turned, he noticed Combs
looking down, which gave the Dutch Brothers employee the opportunity to
draw his gun.

He "realized this was his one chance to survive." The barista "reached
into his front waistband with his right hand and pulled out his Glock .40
caliber handgun. He quickly chambered a round with his left hand and
immediately fired toward Combs. Combs fired his handgun at least twice
toward the worker as the worker continued to fire."

A Lane County jury in March found Plunk not guilty of four felony
charges related to the alleged robbery attempt at the Dutch Brothers coffee
kiosk on Franklin Boulevard.

Plunk testified during his trial that Combs knew the Dutch Brothers
barista and that Combs said he wanted to go to the kiosk to collect money
owed him. He further testified that the barista unlocked the door for

Combs, and that no robbery was planned.

Plunk denied carrying a gun and said the barista shot at him as he rushed toward the kiosk to aid Combs.

Just down the street from where the shooting and robbery took place was a Wendy's restaurant where the investigators say both suspects were seen together. That claim was backed up in court by surveillance video. In the video, both Sirius Combs and Brandon Plunk were seen entering the restaurant about half an hour before the robbery and shooting took place.

Both are seen wearing gloves and dark clothing, and at one point Combs is seen tying a bandana over his face. But Plunk initially told investigators he wasn't with Combs the night of the incident.

The district attorney's office said it believes the video proves Plunk knowingly accompanied Combs—a point Plunk's attorney argued isn't true.

"We felt that it was a direct piece of evidence to establish an association, and again obviously an association contemporaneous with the event in close location," said the Lane Co. District Attorney's Office shortly after Plunk's trial.

The state prosecutor said the video was also important in showing Combs tying a bandana over his face to hide his identity to engage in an activity like a robbery.

The matter with Plunk went to trial. Plunk was acquitted of all charges.

In our classes we teach magic phrases. These are outlined not for bad or wrongful purposes to help bad guys, but to assist the law-abiding citizen who properly holds a concealed handgun license in Oregon getting through the ordeal in the aftermath of a shooting.

Usually in that circumstance the adrenaline has flowed freely. The defensive shooter is either on an adrenaline high or the depressive low after the adrenaline has started leaving the body. There is a blur of thoughts concerning the actions with portions being overlaid. Full clarity of the facts in the aftermath usually only comes after the shooter's body is back in or nearing chemical balance.

While the defensive shooter is in a state of mental disarray, and while his or her body is working to overcome the physical effects of the adrenaline and the factual happenings, this shooter is often confronted with police trying to do what they understand their job to be.

From the contemporary stories above you have learned that in Oregon all shootings resulting in death are initially treated as homicides. More directly they are treated as a murder. It follows that if the defensive shooter knows his or her good work is going to initially be treated as if they were possibly a criminal who had committed a criminal act, they should know how to respond.

We suggest the first words out of the defensive shooter's mouth should be something like, "I was in fear for my life." Or if the circumstances warrant it, "I was in fear for [Third Party's] life." After that one and only statement we suggest as the second and only statement, "I want an attorney." This will be frustrating to enforcement but at that point in time they are not your friend. They think in terms of *you used a gun so you are a bad guy*!

The Law

We start closing this portion of the discussion concerning the use of deadly force printing a small portion of the Oregon Revised Statute for the reader/student's direct review:

> **161.219 Limitations on use of deadly physical force in defense of a person.** Notwithstanding the provisions of ORS 161.209, a person is not justified in using deadly physical force upon another person unless the person reasonably believes that the other person is:
> (1) Committing or attempting to commit a felony involving the use or threatened imminent use of physical force against a person; or
> (2) Committing or attempting to commit a burglary in a dwelling; or
> (3) Using or about to use unlawful deadly physical force against a person. [1971 c.743 §23]
>
> **161.225 Use of physical force in defense of premises.** (1) A person in lawful possession or control of premises is justified in using physical force upon another person when

and to the extent that the person reasonably believes it necessary to prevent or terminate what the person reasonably believes to be the commission or attempted commission of a criminal trespass by the other person in or upon the premises.

(2) A person may use deadly physical force under the circumstances set forth in subsection (1) of this section only:

(a) In defense of a person as provided in ORS 161.219; or

(b) When the person reasonably believes it necessary to prevent the commission of arson or a felony by force and violence by the trespasser.

(3) As used in subsection (1) and subsection (2)(a) of this section, "premises" includes any building as defined in ORS 164.205 and any real property. As used in subsection (2) (b) of this section, "premises" includes any building. [1971 c.743 §25]

161.229 Use of physical force in defense of property. A person is justified in using physical force, other than deadly physical force, upon another person when and to the extent that the person reasonably believes it to be necessary to prevent or terminate the commission or attempted commission by the other person of theft or criminal mischief of property. [1971 c.743 §26]

161.270 Duress. (1) The commission of acts which would otherwise constitute an offense, other than murder, is not criminal if the actor engaged in the proscribed conduct because the actor was coerced to do so by the use or threatened use of unlawful physical force upon the actor or a third person, which force or threatened force was of such nature or degree to overcome earnest resistance.

(2) Duress is not a defense for one who intentionally or recklessly places oneself in a situation in which it is probable that one will be subjected to duress.

(3) It is not a defense that a spouse acted on the command of the other spouse, unless the spouse acted under such co- ercion as would establish a defense under subsection (1) of this section. [1971 c.743 §34; 1987 c.158 §22]

"Shoot the dog!"

Larry is a quiet man; a person most would consider a responsible member of society. He is typical of those who came back from Vietnam. With the horror of those experiences behind him he has led a quiet life. Over time he has become somewhat of a "fix it" kind of guy. Now retired, he takes care of his elderly father, fixes things, shoots shotguns, and of course "shoots" includes "the bull" with the boys at the local commercial breakfast nook.

Judy, Larry's wife, is nearing retirement. She too is quiet, a manager at a local financial institution. Like Larry, she got her Oregon concealed license to carry a handgun about 15 years ago. In putting their lives togeth- er they have earned their way to retirement with a modest estate to help support them in the "golden years."

Larry and Judy would walk their dog through the old grave yard and the new adjoining grave yard, and then return to his father's house each Saturday morning. The whole trip was about two miles of a leisurely time for old friends and lovers to renew.

Their dog Harley, a female cross between American Eskimo and Chow, had aged. She enjoyed the slow meandering walks, never challeng- ing the leash they always kept her on. Larry and Judy were conversing, walking quietly amongst the ancestors of many. The leashed dog was of course doing what older dogs contentedly do.

Unknown to the three of them, a woman and her companion daughter showed up on the other side of the new grave yard with three Rottweilers. They later claimed they did not see Larry or Judy as they turned the dogs loose. We might say dogs being dogs, do what dogs do. Or we might say Rottweilers do what Rottweilers do. In that I guess they are not much different than politicians. They attack the helpless; in this case the initial attack was launched at Harley.

The Rottweilers came running across the grave yard. Larry saw them but did not realize they were in attack mode until the last instant before the actual physical attack was engaged. In his racing mind was the thought, *I cannot believe this is happening.* The initial attack centered on poor old Harley, the leashed dog of Larry and Judy. With bloodlust the now fully engaged Rottweilers gripped Harley in the back and buttocks. Larry jumped on one of the attackers, pulling it off Harley. Judy tried to jump between the dogs that still had a hold on Harley. She was unsuccessful at first. The six ended up rolling on the ground, with the Rotts continuing the attack. Judy kicked one of the Rotts off Harley and the other two women managed to pull the other one off.

It was a melee with Larry and Judy both on the ground under the surprise attack. As they rolled down the gentle slope of the hill side, Larry tried to protect his dog and his wife before he too was overcome by the vicious Rotts. Larry had a difficult time getting the NAA .22 Magnum boot pistol out of the right-hand pocket of his camouflaged winter jacket while rolling on the ground, fighting the dogs and protecting his wife. But he did get it out.

After he got the gun out Judy shouted, "Shoot the dog. Shoot the dog." At that point Judy had a hold of Harley with one arm. Judy was actually on her back, trying to wrap her other arm around the dog she loved. She had also managed to kick one of the dogs away. One of the women jumped on the Rottweiler after Judy kicked it away, and managed to get one of the leashes back on it. The other lady already had one of the Rotts on the ground, actually lying on top of it while trying to bring it under control. That lady, the mother, had lost the leash she started with but had a good hold on the collar and neck skin.

The third Rottweiler had already bit Larry in his gun hand. "Don, one of the problems with the little NAA is that you have to cock it first. I was really having a hard time getting it ready. "He held up his right hand for me to look at as he was talking about what happened. His partially torn finger nail had been stitched back on. I had never seen something like that before. "Why," I asked. Larry answered, "The Doc thought with all of the bites and punctures, that finger nail would be less to have healing at one time, so better for me."

Larry turned thoughtful, then went back to the shooting event. "The dog that had Harley's back and side still in its mouth turned loose and went for Judy's throat. Where we were on the hill at that moment left the other two women behind us, leaving an open field in the direction I had to shoot. I pushed its head away with my left hand as it tried to go for Judy's throat. Her hand was protectively in its mouth." Larry looked at Judy's hand, and the stitches in it before he continued.

"She had her hand in its mouth, trying to keep it from ripping at her throat. I don't know how I had managed to get it cocked, but I put that 22 magnum in the dog's ear." He shrugged. "It didn't even give a yelp. It just folded up. At a glance I could see the other two dogs were still under control."

"At first we didn't even know that Judy or I had been bit. Harley had blood all over her and Judy. We had to take Harley to the vet again today. They put drains in." He looked at Harley standing there with her tail almost bit off at the base, "the doc says she doesn't know whether Harley will make it." Harley had managed to get up and wobble out to the dining area where we were seated. Larry looked at Harley, a sadness in his eyes. The thought weighed on him. He said again, "we don't know yet whether we are going to have to put her down."

As I was interviewing Larry, Judy sat quietly, her lacerated and stitched hand supported by her right, tears in her eyes as she too looked at Harley. She reached down, gently patting the dog she loved so much. Harley tried to wag her tail that had almost been bitten off, whimpered just a little and quit trying to make the wag.

Larry started shaking his head just a little, "Don, I didn't realize. It happened so fast." He took a deep breath. "This has changed my life. I never, *never* expected to ever have to use my gun."

"So what did the cops say when they finally got there?"

Larry went distant, introspective for a moment. He reported the women had left with the two dogs, just loaded them back into the rig. When he realized how bad Harley had been bitten, and that Judy had been bitten too, he calmed her a little, leaving to get his vehicle, three quarters of a mile away.

After calling the Sheriff's Office and reporting the incident he returned to find one of the Sheriff's deputies just arriving. The man was efficient with Larry giving a quick report. The Deputy said nothing about Larry's shooting the Rottweiler.

"I was so worried I would be going to jail or something. I had been told you cannot discharge a firearm for any reason inside of city limits. That is why I hesitated after the attack started and I finally got my gun out."

The Deputy said, "I know who the people are. We have had other dealings with them before. I will follow up."

They loaded Harley in Larry's rig. As they started to leave Somewhere Larry saw the SUV of the two women. He stopped.

"They were nice enough. They offered to pay for everything. We exchanged names." Leaving Somewhere, Larry, Judy, and Harley headed to SomewhereElse, 15 miles away where there are doctors, the veterinarian, and a hospital with emergency room options. While Judy was undergoing emergency treatment, so was Harley.

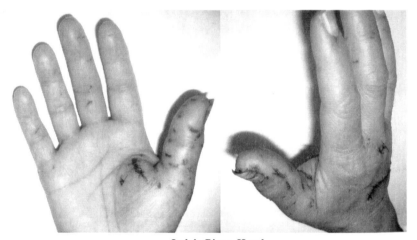

Judy's Bitten Hand

The Sheriff's Office called during the stitching operation, asking a lot more questions.

I think Larry is too kind. He was telling me how these people, the two women, said they didn't see him, Judy, or Harley. The quick immediate question I had was, "Could you see them?"

He could. I reminded him that when they left with their dogs, neither of them offered to give either him or Judy a ride. He had to walk and run all the way back to his father's house the better part of a mile away.

I didn't want to turn Larry to the Dark Side so I stopped with the questioning. I gave him some assurances with the standards of when deadly force is justified in Oregon emphasizing that when a defensive shooter can utter these words based on their reasonable belief he or she is justified: "I feared for my life," or "I feared for the life of another who was in my presence." I suggested that fighting for your life and the life of your wife who is less than six inches away triggers that standard.

This incident points to the reality of most shooting incidents:

1. Most people are mentally NOT prepared to defend themselves or others; and thus,
2. After the confrontation of unlawful felony force being used against them have to take the time to make the decision; and
3. Then after the decision has been made, have to start the physical process of defense; and
4. Only after the first three steps do they become prepared in actuality to defend themselves or others.

It follows the mantra of **Practice, Practice, and Practice** is your friend. In this case Larry would have been well served to have taken his gun out when the danger was first presented rather than trying to dislodge it from his coat while he rolled on the ground. The mantra of **Read, Study, Learn** is also emphasized. Larry had a clear misunderstanding of when and where he could use self-defense. Another unnecessary delay.

Shoot the mosquito! Shoot the mosquito!

I first met Bill in a representation of mining issues almost 20 years ago. Typical of true miners, Bill is independent, well-grounded (no pun intended), and extremely well-educated in spite of having to leave school in the 8th grade. He received one of the last federal mining claim patents granted in Oregon. In his field and the local mining association he belongs to, he is highly respected amongst his peer group.

Bill lives miles and miles beyond the normal conveniences of civilization. The closest commercial electrical power is over 8 miles away. There is no phone. There are no cell towers serving the area. The police and fire department are yet another 21 miles further away. Bill's fire department is a forest fire-fighting water truck that he starts and tests each month. It sets about 60 feet from the house. His police force includes handguns he and Sandy both keep on their persons, as well as AR 15s by the door and a rifle in each vehicle. Their EMTs are Bill and Sandy who have made a study of emergency care. Their ambulance is any of their vehicles.

With all of that as a given, Bill in preparation for the summer mining season (2012) had started preparing to again start water pumps, and various pieces of equipment. That Saturday morning he loaded the new battery for one of the Caterpillars in the back of the pickup, taking it up to the mining operation to change it out.

It was a spring day with a small western Oregon morning drizzle. The soaked ground gave evidence as to why the creek was swollen to its banks. Bill worked on the Cat prepping it to receive the newer battery. At about 10:30 his world was turned upside down, literally. With no warning the stroke was sudden, causing Bill to pass out while he was still standing. He thinks he hit the tailgate of the pickup on his way down, but is not sure whether the sore ribs were from the tail gate or merely hitting the ground.

The impact was twofold, hitting the ground, and second, Bill lost feeling in and use of his left leg and arm. When he came to he was laying partially on his back and left side, the side that had collapsed. The struggle was mighty. He managed to get back up, trying to navigate to the cab of the pickup. He again fell. This time he could not get his leg to work at all even though a little bit of use had come into his left arm and hand. As Bill lay there in the continuing rain he struggled to again see. Things slowly came back into focus. He could see his watch. It was shortly after noon by this time.

Bill's thinking processes were not affected. He tried to get up again and again, but it was no use. One of the experiments in getting back up was to try and rollover so he could get to his hands and knees. He didn't make it, but the rocking back and forth to make the roll caused him to roll the wrong direction, partially pinning the upper portion of his left arm again. The pain was minimal. He wondered whether that was because of the damage of the stroke or he had been lucky in winding up positioned as he was.

Bill laid there, exerting from his energy well to get up, to do something positive to lessen the impacts of what had happened, but all to no avail.

As time passed and Bill did not make it off the hill, Sandy slowly became more and more concerned. It was not like Bill to miss lunch, but sometimes when he was really busy he would.

As Bill lay there he saw the movement, a buzzard flying overhead. Wondering how long he had lain there this time, he watched it circle. As it got closer he mood darkened. Having made the decision, he struggled to get the Smith & Wesson .380 out of his right rear pants pocket. He had five cartridges in the magazine. Another five were in his left front pocket. With a left hand and arm that wasn't working well enough he used his right hand to try to get the extra cartridges out of the pocket. It was slow, working each cartridge up to the mouth of the pocket, and then out onto the ground, but he managed to get the backup ammunition into a small five-cartridge pile where he could get to it without additional difficulty.

The buzzard was still circling, getting lower and lower. Even with the Crimson Trace Laser Sight and the 100 percent overcast sky Bill could not see the red laser dot on the buzzard. Whether it was those first three shots or the movement activity of Bill, the buzzard left, apparently untouched. Bill told me, "With the buzzard getting lower and lower, I was sure I was dying. After all, that is what buzzards eat, isn't it. Imagine my relief when it flew away!" We all laughed at the joking retelling there in the hospital room but part of the seriousness showed through Bill's ready laugh and eyes.

The attack on Bill did not stop. He settled back in to the wait, knowing if he did not show up for dinner Sandy would surely come for him. Even though Bill had lost most of the use of his left hand, he had not lost feeling. He looked down in response to the prickling sensation. The irony of the tiny mosquito sucking his blood was not lost on him as he thought, It's going to be a mosquito, not a buzzard, that eats me. With the Crimson Laser Sight recently on his mind, he wondered and put the pondering thought into action. When the laser sight red dot touched the mosquito, it flew away.

That single mosquito turned into more. Bill wondered, "They are winged. Would a bunch of them be a herd, flock, covey, or just what are they called." The next thought was, "Simple enough, blood suckers." That brought his thoughts to being eaten alive, which brought him to thinking about bear, cougar, and wolves. He took a break from the ponderings and wonderings to reload the magazine with his good hand.

After the experience of going down was over, after the rescue, he pondered the Oregon licensed concealed handgun. It had protected him from a carrion eater, wild insects, and gave him peace of mind as he considered his damaged placement on the food chain. Bill lives in a portion of the state that is known for its bear, cougar, and wolves. But most important, after the search started and was headed the wrong direction on the claim, when he heard the searchers, the "Pow!" of the little .380 summoned help.

• Sometimes the sound of the gun is enough.

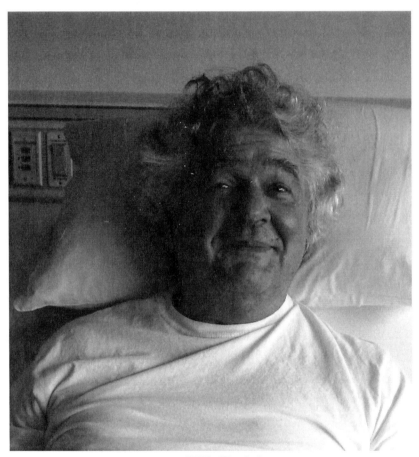

Bill in Hospital

Trayvon Martin

Trial by Media or Learn the Facts after the Fact.

Our criminal justice system in Oregon is designed to protect people who are charged with a crime in a small multitude of ways. First, the arresting person or police have to believe the person being arrested is in fact guilty of a crime. If it is a citizen's arrest, then the arresting citizen has to actually have seen the crime committed. If it is the police making the arrest, then they have to have a "probable cause" to believe the person being arrested committed the crime.

After the arrest and depending on the seriousness of the alleged "crime" there will be a determination by either the District Attorney's office or an indictment from a grand jury before formal charges are filed and the matter is brought before a judge.

The next step is a period of "discovery" where each side gets to look at the evidence of the other. This is to eliminate "trial by ambush" where one side either holds crucial evidence to the last minute or hides evidence altogether in order to alter the outcome of a "fair" trial.

Last, the alleged criminal has to be proven guilty by the state under an umbrella of further safeguards which include the finding of guilty has to be by a standard of "beyond a reasonable doubt." Arriving at a determination of whether the accused is guilty is accomplished by a jury of his or her peers, a jury disassociated from the system. In the interest of justice and to protect the rights of the accused, that jury is usually 12 persons.

That brief outline brings us to events on national television in the evening of March 27, 2012. Unfortunately the subject matter of the event was not a new experience of the media, only the application. A national television station had taken a poll based on the question, "Do you think George Zimmerman should be arrested." The response was: 73 percent Yes; 11 percent No; 16 percent Undecided.

This triggered many of my buttons, especially as an attorney no longer in the work stream. So I researched who George Zimmerman is[12] and what the circumstances were that would lead to this kind of concern. The following is what I learned:

Trayvon Martin (17) was shot and killed by a Neighborhood Watch captain George Zimmerman (28). From that incident have been town hall meetings, protests, and rallies. Zimmerman claims he shot young Mr. Martin in self-defense.

There are police reports saying Mr. Martin was the aggressor on February 26, 2012 knocking Zimmerman to the ground with a single punch and then climbing on top of the Neighborhood Watch captain and slamming the back of Zimmerman's head into the ground. At least one witness reportedly told the police that he saw Martin on top of Zimmerman, striking the man, while Zimmerman called out for help.

Added into this factual morass police say Zimmerman was bleeding from the nose, had a fat lip, and confirmed the back of Zimmerman's head was cut.

Zimmerman told police he spotted Martin heading toward the grocery store. When he spotted Martin he called the police to report a black youth acting suspiciously, possibly on drugs. Zimmerman then stepped out of his SUV to follow Martin, even though dispatch told him he didn't need to do so.

Zimmerman told the police he had lost sight of Martin and was heading back to his car when the youth suddenly stepped into his path. According to a local paper Martin asked Zimmerman if he had a problem. Zimmerman said "no" and reached for his cell phone. Martin then said something like, "Well, you do now" and punched him, according to the local newspaper's sources.

The other side of this factual evidence coin are the claims of family and friends, that Mr. Martin was a model student, with good grades, and has never had problems. They claim the police and news media are involved in a campaign of "blame-the-victim" reporting.

Into this factual pizza of many ingredients came information that possibly Trayvon Martin was not the model student citizen the family would like everyone to believe he was. It was reported that Mr. Martin was in his father's city of Sanford, Florida because he had been suspended for 10 days from his Miami high school after the remains of Marijuana were found in a plastic bag in the teenager's book bag.

The first real trial on these facts started with President Obama's political comments about a matter in which he spoke so prematurely as to make his comments an embarrassment to his office and party. Various other politicians weighed in on the subject matter with Ds primarily on one side of the issue, Rs on the other side.

More importantly, the media also weighed in, painting this tragic circumstance in terms of racial responses by the white, vigilante captain Zimmerman against the helpless and defenseless, perfect person of black heritage, Trayvon Martin. But before I castigate the news media too much, they are trying to survive in an age going digital, trying to do their part to financially survive while facing substantial losses as an industry due to the impacts of the modern day footprint of wireless, e-books, blogs, and the list goes on and on. From the incident outlined to this point, days have passed and I again visited the Internet.

At this time Zimmerman has been arrested. The charge for which he had already been found guilty by judgment of the media is second degree Murder.

I do not attempt to overlay this example with the appropriate Florida law. Instead, for our understanding we apply Oregon law. For a determination of whether, under these facts as they are currently understood, Captain Zimmerman is guilty or not guilty of some form of murder will hinge on whether the jury would ultimately believe Captain Zimmerman had a reasonable belief he was justified in using deadly force against an attacker who was using unlawful force against him; a force by Martin that was intended or likely to cause death or serious bodily injury, and therefore of whether Zimmerman's deadly response was justified.

There is wisdom in remembering for the Zimmerman/Martin scenarios of the world a full gathering of the facts helps in making a determination of which side of the fence we personally really want to be on; that is, if we want to be on the fence at all.

There is another layer of added wisdom in remembering and understanding that if we are involved in a shooting, the first words out of our mouths should be, "I feared for my life." The second group of words out of our mouths should be, "I want an attorney."

But the real question for us, for you and for me is whether we would want to be ultimately tried by a group of our peers, 12 persons charged with some of the most serious decision-making who will be allowed to hear all of the facts in an environment designed to protect our rights as well as the alleged victims; or the alternative?

And here is what the alternative really is: In the event of a handgun discharge where you are the person who pulled the trigger, do you want to be tried in the media and by the media? Do you want to be tried by popular vote? Do you want your life torn apart by the evidence gatherers called "news" reporters? Do you want to be tried by public opinion where you are painted by the broad black (as it is used here I mean the color of the paint, not the skin) brush of political correctness? Lest you misunderstand the core of these questions, do you want to run the risk of being found guilty by a prosecutor, a judge, and a jury who's true goal and ambition is to financially survive in the face of their challenge by the new digital social and news media?

The same question presented in a simpler format: Given a choice of only one of two allowed possibilities: Do you want to be tried by a media organization who's true motive is to sell news or do you want to be tried by a system designed to protect your individual rights?

How does the Martin/Zimmerman happenings relate to you? If you are the one who becomes involved in a deadly force defensive shooting, it could ultimately mean you being tried by the press, and/or the current political machine of "correctness" notwithstanding whatever the true facts may be.

The Ox-Bow Incident is a 1943 film directed by William Wellman starring Henry Fonda and a host of others who over time became well-known in movies. This movie is taken from the 1940 western novel by Walter Clark. It depicts democracy in action when the protections in our criminal system are ignored.

- Justified force that is a deadly force by a person in response to unlawful force which is authorized when the intent or likely outcome of the confrontation is death or serious bodily harm, but the person using a justified response may only use the degree of force which the person believes is reasonable under the circumstances.

- Deadly force can be used in self-preservation or the defense of a third party in the defendant's presence where the third party is the object of unlawful force likely or intended to cause death or serious bodily injury.

- In situations where a person has engaged in a mutual combat, a person is NOT justified in the use of force rising to a level of deadly force as a means to end the conflict.
- In Oregon every justified (deadly) force situation is investigated as if the defensive shooter committed a crime.
- To use defensive deadly force otherwise called "self-defense," the defendant must reasonably believe their response is justified because the attacker engaged in an unlawful physical force.
- That "reasonable belief" usually will be tested by a judge, jury, and/or a District Attorney.
- Sometimes the reasonable belief has to be become the defensive shooter's reality in only fractions of a second.
- "I feared for my life," is worth knowing and using; or
- "I was in fear for third party's life."
- "I want an attorney before any further questioning," is also worth knowing and using.
- A deadly force justified response is authorized only for as long as it takes to eliminate the threat of the wrongful felony force being used against the defensive shooter or a third party the defensive shooter is protecting.

CHAPTER 3

Reasonable

Recommended reading: *The Founders' Second Amendment* by Stephen Halbrook.[13]

One of the issues each of us must come to grips with in such a way that we have clarity in understanding is about when self-defense is authorized. Like hand-in-glove, when self-defense or deadly force is justified is tested by what is reasonable under the circumstances. Did you or I or another have a set of circumstances that triggered our right to self-defense or the defense of another with deadly force?

To weigh the circumstance that involves the unlawful physical use of force intended or likely to cause death or serious bodily injury against us appears simple enough on its face. Where the system breaks down is that the judge and/or jury get to hear and analyze those facts sometimes over a period of days or even months, while we may only have decision-making moments.

If we choose life, which includes self-defense with a deadly force response, would that response be ruled justifiable under Oregon laws? Each fact pattern is unique. Each circumstance will flow with and be weighed against the standards found in the Oregon Revised Statutes.

A Philosophy of Enlightenment

As our experiences are compounded over time we see Democrats become Republicans and Republicans become Democrats. People change their religions. In the family we see younger siblings treated differently than the older children as their parents come into new understandings of how to raise a child. We learn that with experience sometimes comes wisdom and tempering. It is an observable common fact that in compelling traumatic experience often comes growth. The more traumatic the experience, the greater the growth.

A friend's son-in-law came back from war this last fall. As we sat around the hunting camp fire he was reflecting on his soon to be 21st birthday. Like most war veterans what he did not want to talk about was what it was really like in a war zone. John—and yes, that really is his name this time—was reflecting on what it was like coming "home" to a wife he had missed for almost a year, a new son he did not see born, a new house, a car he did not own when he left for the Middle East, and many other changes in that 12 month period.

We, the "older" folks, listened as we all gazed into the depths of the dancing late night camp fire. What was puzzling to John was how he could be old enough and responsible enough to kill "rag heads" with a multimillion dollar piece of equipment in a land far away, but he still had to wait another 18 days before he would responsible enough to drink alcohol in Oregon.

John expressed his lack of understanding how he could be responsible enough to vote for the political assignment of the most powerful person in the world, the President of the United States of America, but now as a law-abiding citizen he has to have a license to carry a concealed handgun, a license he could not even make an application for another 18 days. As John was verbalizing his pondering for general considerations, he speculated on why a government, Oregon in this case, would really care. He wondered how many of the politicians had actually paid their dues, dues of the same type he had paid, and he may yet again have to pay.

Those of us as "older Vietnam Era folks" around the camp fire had pondered the same things when we were that age. That type of reasoning took me back to law school. There in the halls of legal academia I too got caught up in the repeated musing and wonderment of my youth.

With six children and a job prosecuting for Oregon OSHA, I had taken on other responsibilities as well. I had run for and been elected to the highest student government political office, Student Bar Association President. As such, I found that I had become a parent of not only my 6 children, but over 400 young adults. My wife was holding down three jobs, managing our household affairs, and doing the nurturing thing with the kids so we could financially survive the experience and be responsible parents.

Into this busy lifestyle I was learning law and the public policy that drove the law at that time. Like John, I had pondered some of the mysteries of government when I was younger and was now again on that path, but with a changing perspective as my understanding of the law and "public policy" was being changed. One of the questions that came to mind was with the almost obscene amount of money spent on the loss of lives and property (vehicles) on the freeways, highways, and byways of the various states here in the United States: Why doesn't government just slow the traffic down? What if we had a maximum speed limit of 20 miles per hour? After all, isn't the purpose of government under our social compact, to protect us?

As I speculated on the "what if" of such happenings and the potential impacts, I realized that slowing traffic might not be good for business. In the middle of such reoccurring thoughts I had an experience unfold around me in my Civil Law class. The discussion that day dealt with administrative agencies, how their governing laws are created, and the focus of those laws. We were talking about the child welfare systems in the various states and the governmental view of the necessity for protection of children generally and to protect them from their parents.

The class went backwards in history to early Anglo-Saxon laws and views. Children were property under the control of their parents. Springing forward to modern governments—and I am making giant leaps in this few sentence summary: Government today recognizes a "state interest" in your children and my children, (take a significant pause) **as a human resource for government**. From that interest is derived the justification for governmental interference in the lives of so many.

The light bulb of enlightenment flashed on, perhaps for only the briefest of time, but even so I got it. Having taken this short bird-walk, I turn back to what I hinted this chapter is really about, what "reasonable" is.

When we read the definitions in the world of concealed handgun carry laws we keep coming back to the concept of making "reasonable" choices in life and death split second, decision-making circumstances. Far too often a judge or jury with a huge amount of information we did not have at the time we were making the decision will decide whether our decision was "reasonable."

Oregon has built into this process sever limitations on the evidence that is allowed into this process, evidence that could be most important to us as a society, and to you and to me as individuals. For example, if the bad guy were someone generally known in the community to be a bad guy, that would not be allowed into evidence even though it may be a part of your or my decision-making process. It is Oregon's view that for this kind of "trial" the only issues allowed are those surrounding our decision in a clean and pure environment. It does not matter we might have believed that upon the bad guy's reputation, the actions of the bad guy were the kind of force contemplated in the statute.

So the bad guy says, "I am going to kill you." He reaches around behind himself and before you or I see the handgun or knife, we draw and shoot. The fact that the bad guy always carries a gun or knife and that he has used it before may be excluded from the world of evidence because it is too highly prejudicial. The question becomes, did he have a gun or knife this time?

For these facts we are going to go with, he did not. So now the judge or jury is faced with making a decision based not on the fact that the bad guy was a bad guy and most probably did have a gun or knife. The judge/jury will be asking in some form this question; would a prudent person faced with a bad guy who merely said "I am going to kill you," be justified in using a deadly force response when the reality was the bad guy had no gun and no knife?

With this said, and with the other discussion to this point, we look at Federal House Bill 822, 2011 as represented to me and others by email from the NRA on October 15, 2011and by email on March 14, 2012 from the NRA and which we have learned has passed the federal senate:

"H.R. 822, introduced in the U.S. House by Representatives Cliff Stearns (R-Fla.) and Heath Shuler (D-N.C.), would allow any person with a valid state-issued concealed firearm permit to carry a concealed firearm in any state that issues concealed firearm permits, or that does not prohibit the carrying of concealed firearms for lawful purposes. A state's laws governing where concealed firearms may be carried would apply within its borders. The bill applies to D.C., Puerto Rico and U.S. territories. It would not create a federal licensing system; rather, it would require the states to recognize each others' carry permits, just as they recognize drivers' licenses and carry permits held by armored car guards. Rep. Stearns has introduced such legislation since 1995.

H.R. 822 recognizes the significant impact of the landmark cases, District of Columbia v. Heller (2008) and McDonald v. City of Chicago (2010), which found that the Second Amendment protects a fundamental, individual right to keep and bear arms and that the protections of the Second Amendment extend to infringements under state law."

While we are highly supportive of the NRA and believe everyone who loves the concepts of freedom should seriously consider joining the NRA at the national level, the NRA misses the boat on this one. The Second Amendment is a guarantee against the encroachment of the federal government on our individual right to keep and bear arms. Part of the purpose of that guarantee is so that we can defend ourselves from our own government if necessary.

Article 1 Section 27 of the Oregon Constitution is our state making a similar guarantee to us under our social compact at the more local level. We shall and do have the right to bear arms for the defense of ourselves, and the State....

And to the Federal Second Amendment: "*A well regulated Militia, being necessary to the security of a free State, the right of the people to keep and bear arms, shall not be infringed.*"

To further this discussion we look at the difference between reciprocity and recognition among the various states: Simply put, reciprocity means to have a formal agreement between the states. Recognition means that one state will recognize the action of another state. In this case the concealed license recognition will be mandated. If that were to happen under the current outline in HB 822, each state will apply its own laws for the carrying of concealed handguns.

HB 822 would overlay recognition and/or reciprocity upon the several states as a matter of law, leaving to each state the right to control how its own state gun laws apply. Talk about a mess. Since the core or body of the state laws would apply under HB 822 we only need to look to the absurdity of one situation to understand the absurdity of it all.

You have been traveling through Nevada, but have stopped at Too Tall Casino for a brief moment of fun. You were lucky. You won and walked out with $5,000 of new money. So, you think you have something because you were in the state of Any, and your concealed handgun license in Any state is good in, say Nevada under federal HB 822. As you are going back to the state of Any you are stopped for a non-arrestable infraction in Nevada. What you do not have on you because your state did not require it is a card showing you are proficient with the particular personal protection handgun you are carrying concealed. In your state you don't have to tell the police anything about your license or the fact you have a gun.

After the stop and a minor confrontation with the officer of which laws should apply, you are arrested. The initial charge was illegal carrying of a loaded concealed handgun. With a license from the state of Any that doesn't fully work in Nevada, you pay the fines and whatnot before going on your merry way. The impound fee is $850. The fines are $1,750.00. The misdemeanor charge is everlasting. The attorney who convinced you to plea out because you don't have the $350,000 or so to take this matter to the Federal Supreme Court only cost you $7,500. Of course you lost your job because your employment does not allow employment of criminals as a condition of your employment. On the plus side you had $5,000 new money to apply to the process only leaving you $4,100 in the hole with no job.

The reality under constitutional law where states join the greater

"United" compact is a legal theory not advanced by the NRA, yet more foundationally correct on a national basis. When a state joins the Union, the Union recognizes the constitutional social compact of that state. Thus, each state of the union recognizes that compact. In its simplest form each state recognizes the right of the joining states' citizens to carry, and that is at a federal level.

The NRA and many others take a path that infringes on the Federal Constitutional 10th Amendment of States Rights. However, with all of that said, we await the ultimate decision of the current process which has been bogged down in the Senate since November of 2011. By the time this book is published this matter may be settled, but we doubt it.

The good part for me is that for all of those from other states who would carry in Oregon under HB 822, they need to read this book. Ah-h-h, a national market place for my work!

Out-of-state Permit – First Glimpse

Idaho resident John Smith with a Utah non-resident carry and conceal permit was traveling on the back roads of Pandora, Oregon during deer hunting season. On a late Wednesday afternoon, cool and bright with very few clouds for the time of year in Eastern Oregon, John and his wife Jane approached a general stop by Oregon Fish and Wildlife at an outback rural crossroads reporting station manned by the ODFW and State Police Officer 1 (OSPO1). John and Jane were asked at the stop if they had filled their deer-hunting tags. They were told this was necessary information for various studies and reporting purposes to allow the Oregon Department of Fish and Wildlife better management of the King's deer, or something like that.

Mr. Smith was polite and respectful. ODFW personally wanted to see his out-of-state tag and hunting license. Mr. Smith told the ODFW representatives he did not have one. He said he was not hunting, just visiting friends in their hunting camp. In the process he noted to the ODFW consistent with the NRA recommendations that he had a concealed permit and handgun. He went on to say again he was not hunting, just visiting family and camping in the woods at the hunting location of the family. Mrs. Smith told the ODFW representatives their daughters, both teenagers, were back at the camp now and they, the parents, had just come out to get groceries.

The ODFW worker called OSPO1 over, telling her of the conversation and about the possibility of a concealed handgun. The officer respectfully inquired.

The handgun, a Springfield .40XD was in the console of the big truck. OSPO1 asked the Smiths to "exit the vehicle and stand right over there," pointing a little away from the crewed cab F250 Ford. She took the gun, a Glock 17, and checked it. The magazine was full and there was a cartridge in the chamber. Under Utah law, both are allowed if the occupants have a valid concealed carry handgun license. I have no idea what Idaho law allows.

1) In Oregon (which recognizes no other states at this time) the non-resident Utah permit was and is not a valid license to carry concealed. 2) In Oregon one cannot carry a concealed loaded handgun unless they have a valid Oregon Concealed Handgun License. At that time and at this time that means that there can be no cartridges in the handgun. (See the ATV section for an exception.)

The officer could have arrested both because in the course of the on-site investigation it was determined that Mrs. Smith also knew the handgun was in the console and it was as accessible to her as it was to Mr. Smith. The officer was apologetic in the arrest noting, "If it [the Glock 17] wasn't loaded, I would have just given you a warning."

Where I lived at that time anyone within two or three miles were considered neighbors. My neighbors who were family of Mr. Smith were literally on my door step Thursday morning wanting to know if I could do anything for Mr. Smith. The story from here gets longer and convoluted but we move forward to a point in time after my discussions with the DA.

Whether in the interests of interstate relations, or for some other reason, the DA immediately made the decision to treat the matter as a violation instead of a misdemeanor. That meant a get-out-of-jail *almost* free card. Mr. Smith did not have to come back to Oregon for trial. I made the plea of "no contest" for him; next paying the fine out of money he left in my Client Trust Fund, and saw to the conclusion of the paperwork.

What most people don't understand is that the federal Second Amendment is a guarantee only against the intrusions of the federal government. Where there is no governmental intrusion, there is no need for federal involvement unless people are being denied their right to be able to defend themselves with force of arms (Oregon). The quicksand of surrounding discussions fills many books and endless hours of debate in the halls of Congress[14] and the media.

Ignoring those discussions, and bringing this outlined issue home to those of us in Oregon; our Oregon Constitution is more directed toward us individually. We recognize as a part of our social compact at Article I, Section 27 the dual responsibility to protect ourselves and the state. In that recognition, we make sure we have the ability to do so by reserving that fundamental right to us not only as protection against the wrongful acts of the state, but also to protect ourselves from the wrongful acts of others. To the best of my knowledge, none of us have waived that right except by being adjudicated a felon or crazy.

Our Legislature has placed boundaries so we can more easily understand when protection in the form of self-defense is socially acceptable. In doing so the state is trying to draw upon the commonality of the human experience where we collectively say through our representatives we want to be able to defend ourselves but we do not accept that defense as license to be abusive even unto death of another without justifiable cause.

As this circle of the discussion on the smaller scale comes to closure, what we see is a number of competing interests, surrounding issues of when we can use the justification of deadly force in defense of ourselves from the unlawful use of physical force against us or others in our presence; or the use of self-defense against other physical force that is likely to cause serious bodily injury.

Part of what we come to understand is the decision we have to make in the briefest moment in time will most probably be tested against the reasonably prudent person standard as discussed above. That decision will be scrutinized by others with the time to inquire fully and make their own independent decision of whether we really were authorized to use deadly force against the unlawful physical force being used against us.

The "fairness" of this process, while in some instances suspect, is all that we have separating us from some form of anarchy.

Given that HB 822 referred above is in the process of determining whether it, or some modified version of it, will become the law for reciprocity and recognition between the various states: Until then we live with the current system which includes Oregon's refusal to accept non-resident concealed handgun licenses.

My belief in the #1 Reason for having a non-resident Utah Concealed Permit

Thus, we look toward Utah and ask why so many people get a non-resident Utah Handgun License. Over time a non-resident Utah license has gained a growing following of states willing to either engage in reciprocity agreements with Utah or in one of the alternatives, willing to simply recognize the Utah Concealed Handgun License. Under the umbrella of a "reciprocity" agreements, whichever state's laws are applicable are agreed to formally.

Utah's Bureau of Criminal Identification has processed and granted the following number of concealed firearm licenses:

2006 15,696
2007 29,353
2008 44,891
2009 73,925
2010 67,263
2011 76,239

As a side note: I called the Oregon State Police on March 15, 2012 to see how many Oregon concealed handgun licenses were issued in 2011. I was informed concealed handgun licensing is a function of the 36 counties, not the state. It was suggested if I want that information, I would need to contact each of the 36 counties to see how many licenses they issued. We return to Utah.

With a defensive shooting situation where the defensive shooter has a Utah handgun license, it is arguable that Utah laws should govern a shooting incident that comes out of the laws governing the recognized, licensed, non-resident defensive shooter. Conceptually and simply stated: If a defensive shooter is acting under the Utah laws as he or she knows them in carrying a concealed handgun granted by Utah, then that person should be allowed to use the laws of Utah in a defensive shooting. Of course there are strong views on both sides of this offering.

The thrust of the immediately previous discussion is a judge or jury often gets to determine in Oregon whether the defensive shooting was in fact justified in some theory of self-defense or defense of others. To do so the act of self-defense as "reasonable" is explored.

What we have already learned is that in making that split second determination based on the immediacy of a necessary response the defensive shooter's burden is sometimes a very heavy. In addressing the "reasonableness" coming to a conclusion a deadly force response is justified can be even more weighty in part because the rules of evidence in Oregon are restrictive with respect to what the judge/jury is allowed to consider when making their decision of what a reasonable and prudent person would do. It is tough in an after-the-fact shooting to look at and weigh fairness.

If at this juncture it sounds like I am about to advocate a defensive shooter should have no limitations and that he or she should not be held to some standard of reasonableness, I am not. The question turns on what, from an evidentiary stand point, should be allowed for purview[15] by the trier-of-fact.

We use the following slide supplied to us by the Bureau of Criminal Identification, State of Utah:

Justification of Force

Considerations in determining reasonableness of force

- Nature of danger
- Immediacy of danger
- Probability that unlawful force would result in death or serious bodily injury
- Prior violent acts or propensities
- Patterns of abuse or violence

What this slide teaches us is that whether the judge or jury in Utah, the trier-of-fact is allowed to look at the entirety of the potential evidence package for a determination of what may be considered reasonable. Included in that review are the prior violent acts or propensities of the parties, and the patterns of abuse or violence of the parties. What this means is that we as law-abiding citizens who have good and clean records get measured against the Bad Guy and his or her record. As a historical aside: Originally juries of peers were the people of the community. They often already knew of the propensities of both the good guys and the bad guys.

In many of the states their rules of evidence do not allow some level of "probability" the unlawful physical force would result in death or serious bodily injury. The public policy reason for this is the system is geared for resolution of the crime after it has been committed. It follows speculative material is not admissible because it unfairly prejudices the trier-of-fact.

When observed in its totality, this slide from the Utah presentation is why personally I think Utah evidentiary laws should apply for all of us who carry non-resident Utah Concealed Handgun licenses in other states that recognize or have reciprocity agreements with Utah. If the reciprocity agreements have language in them that do not allow the benefit of letting the judge/jury weigh all of the relevant facts in determining how bad the bad guy really is, then the self-defensive shooter is being done a disservice by the very government designed to protect him or her and those he or she would protect. We move on.

The #2 reason for having a Utah Concealed Handgun Permit
Reciprocity and Recognition
Staying out of Trouble

The observable fact gleaned from a large number of people who have taken our class is that most of them are more mature, probably over 70 percent. And "yes," I am being kind to those of us who are older. The simple fact is a lot of us as we reach the golden[16] years like to travel. For many of us weighing every bit as strongly as personal protection, is the "insurance" policy a non-resident Utah permit gives us in our travels from state to state as a protection from governmental interference in our lives under the mantel of enforcement.

While the governmental commentary may be sad, the general expressed truth is that as we become freer to travel, we want less hassle from government. We do not want to worry about whether in one state our motor home will be considered a "residence" but in another it is a "vehicle." We do not want to have to worry about whether the handgun on the back shelf or in the drawer will be considered "concealed." We simply do not want the hassle of dealing with enforcement. So we get a Utah (and Arizona) non-resident permit that is wildly recognized by most states.

We have current maps at www.oregonconcealedlaw.com demonstrating a visual view of those states that either have reciprocity with or recognize the non-resident Utah Concealed Handgun Permit, Arizona, and Oregon. With the Oregon, Utah, and Arizona license to carry concealed you can plan your trip through those recognition and reciprocal states without having to worry about whether your handgun might be considered concealed. We caution the reader as you study these maps not to rely on them. The various laws of the various states change much faster than do revisions of books or web sites. Therefore, in the reasonable planning of your travels you should design your routes and then review the various concealed laws of those states you plan to travel through.

As a personal choice due to political and practical reality whereby we are not allowed to be able to protect ourselves, we do not visit or spend money in California or Colorado. In becoming internet business we also use the internet for much of our business. It also follows and the simple fact is we do not deal with internet businesses that have California or Colorado business addresses.

Remembering Oregon applies the "accessibility" standard to whether one has access to and therefore control of a concealed handgun, we believe both a husband and wife, or other relationships that often travel together should all at a minimum have the Oregon concealed carry authorizations in Oregon. It relieves a lot of stress and hassle for in-state travel.

- Plan your interstate travel. Then look up the various "concealed" laws of the states you plan to travel through.
- Get an Oregon, Utah, and Arizona permit to relieve enforcement hassles during interstate travel.

CHAPTER 4

!Safety! – !Children! – !Safety!

About Children Safety

Perhaps the most important discussion in this work—*child safety*—needs our serious attention. I was conducting some business in early November of 2008 in Redding, California where I met with Lowell Fletcher. Lowell teaches a wide range of NRA courses, First Aid, and other safety related matters. We were standing outside of the local Elks Lodge when we saw a funeral procession. In my personal observations over the years it was the longest one I had or have ever personally seen. Of course, it was a solemn event. Lowell stood with his right hand across his heart.

"Who was it?" The question was asked quietly because I was deep in thought. In these matters, respect is certainly called for.

"Jason's son. He was four."

We stood, almost at attention as the long procession continued. After a bit Lowell added more, "He was climbing a bookcase in his father's bed room. It came over and the gun on the top shelf hit the floor, discharging." Lowell paused, as if he were done.

"So, tell me more," I asked.

Lowell shook his head just a little, more of a negative nod. "Well, they really don't know much and no one is talking right now. Lots of speculation, but no one knows for sure."

The death of anyone seems to always be a sad time, but the death of a child can weigh heavily on family, friends, and a community. There is something special about children. Perhaps it is their closeness to innocence we all wish we still had. I reflected on my own children and grandchildren having sobering thoughts. The death of my adult brother over 30 years ago still weighs on my mother. Regardless of age our children are always just that, our children.

For the next few days I watched the Internet news trying to search out more information. The child was the son of a Redding Police Officer, Jason Rhoads. None of the reports I read said which of the parents were home at the time of the accident, but they were all clear that one of the parents was home. Apparently there was another child at home as well. One of the reports noted that it was the father's service handgun. The "service" was the Redding police force.

Given this limited information I speculate the parent at the house was the father because his service weapon was there but I don't know and it does not really matter.

For the purposes of our classes when we present the NRA safety portion on children I reflect to my class on this incident. I teach it the way Lowell taught it to me.

We are taught in the Basic Pistol Instructors class to emphasize child safety. We teach that best practice is to keep all guns, except those on your person secured. Trigger locks and barrel locks at a minimum should be used. A child should be taught if they see a gun NOT to touch it. They should immediately go to an adult and tell the adult of the gun.

At Oregon Concealed we advocate having a secure gun safe if it is at all possible. It is not enough to have the gun safe; it needs to be used for all guns, all of those not being carried for personal protection.

Second to this is the safe transportation of guns. Except for the personal gun(s) being carried for personal protection, transported guns should be safely secured. With care they should be put in a transportation device (carrying case, trunk, etc.) and taken out with care. Child safety starts with us, not the children.

Bird walk

Jerry Webber was a member of the SWAT team, a valued member of the police force in Eugene, Oregon and a valued member of his community. He had given presentations at high schools and the University of Oregon on responsible gun ownership and safety in addition to his duties as a member of the SWAT team. In February of 2011, in spite of his training and background he had an accidental discharge, a shooting that killed him.

He was going to the range with a friend to get in some practice with his hunting rifle. Even with all his training and background, he made the mistake that day of storing a loaded firearm for transportation. He further failed to engage safe practices while taking the hunting rifle out of the vehicle which led to the discharge that killed him.

The thrust of this short bird walk is to note that even the best of the good guys make mistakes. So what chance does a child have around us when we fail to engage truly safe actions for and in their behalf?

For the purposes of safety, and the impacts this can have on an individual, especially concerning children, this is the place to talk about a few more safety rules. We teach that **every gun is loaded**. It is to be treated as loaded at all times. We talked earlier about when a gun is cleared. Even after the exercise and you know whether the handgun is loaded, treat it as if it is. Knowing the handgun is going to be treated as loaded do not put it in the hands of unsupervised children.

All of us know that if the **muzzle is kept pointed in a safe direction**, even in the event of an accidental discharge, no one is going to get hurt.

The Accident

I bought one of the early Glock 17s when they were first made available to the general public. I was amazed at how easily it was to take apart for cleaning. The early manual said to disassemble it into the basic four units, barrel, slide, housing, and magazine. Put the barrel, slide, and housing into the dishwasher on "hot." Wash it. Take it out immediately after washing. Put half a drop of "fine" oil on each side of the slide. Lightly oil the barrel if desired, but the manual noted it was not necessary. Reassemble.

Good friends, Billy and Sandy Smith, had come over for a visit. We were sitting around the kitchen table, Billy across from me. Sandy was at the head of the table away from the wall. My wife was beside Sandy, on my right. "Read this." I handed Billy the manual. While he was reading I took the 17 out of the shoulder holster, dropped the magazine out, and took the cartridge out of the chamber. At all times I kept the muzzle pointed in a safe direction.

Then I took it apart. For whatever reason, perhaps like a child that wants to impress the adults, I was anxious. I had some difficulty in breaking the pistol down. Even as simple as it is to do, it just didn't go right. After several tries I got the slide off (kept forgetting to pull the trigger for the release). Billy was appropriately impressed and humored. With tongue-in-cheek he asked, "Have you read the manual?"

In my growing frustration I ignored him. I reassembled the gun. What I did not notice in my continued and growing angst was that I had failed to get the slide down on the side away from my body.

Billy pointed, "Don. Your slide is not on right."

I looked. Sure enough, Billy was correct on that one. I don't know how I reassembled the Glock that way. I have tried since then so many times to understand how it is possible to get the slide in that position, but to no avail. I was having an almost impossible time again removing the slide. But at almost the moment I was going to give up it came off. My embarrassment was high but my escalating frustration was even higher.

By way of explanation but not for excuse, my mental hold on the situation had slipped. All I wanted to accomplish at that moment was to get that gun back together and go on to something else. Without further thought when the slide went on so easily compared to everything else I worked the mechanism, never giving the slightest thought to the fact I had just reinstalled the magazine and chambered a live cartridge.

At all times, as a trained and habitual safety precaution I had kept the Glock pointed away from everyone. Without further thought I put it under my left arm to maximize the positive effect of keeping the gun pointed safely. To let the pressure off the firing mechanism with the Glock the only way I know is to pull the trigger. I did.

The hot case from the now discharged firearm married itself to my underarm. With the pain that caused I thought I had shot myself. I wanted to pee, crap, and puke in that moment that seemed to stand still. With the adrenalin flow, I looked at Billy. The shock on his and Sandy's face was the same. The only difference in Linda's look was that as the wife I know she felt compelled to say something. Her mouth was working like a guppy out of water but no words were coming out.

To compound the now ultimate embarrassment of the moment Billy said, "I was watching. I just didn't believe you were going to pull the trigger."

"Well, Bill, I wish you would have said something. At least I kept it pointed away from everyone the whole time. I guess..." There wasn't really any more for me to say so I didn't say more.

Billy repeated, "I was watching." Nodding and pointing he said, "Take the mag out and the live round. Then let's survey the damage."

The speeding 9mm bullet had gone through both sides of the wall, through the back of the clothes dryer, out the front door of the clothes dryer, through the opposite wall of the utility room, and made a furrow in the lawn about 30 inches in length before hitting a rock and ricocheting.

I feel for the family of Officer Webber. I personally know how easy it can be to drop our guard for just a moment, to get caught up in the circumstances surrounding us.

In my accidental discharge we were more than just "lucky." Because of a learned habit of safe practices developed with the shooting of tens of thousands of rounds, even though I failed in this one instance by having an unplanned accidental discharge, we were protected through the application of trained and ingrained safety rules.

Some of the later humor that came out of this is derived from the third general safe practice rule. **Be certain of the target and what is beyond it.** It is certainly arguable I missed on this one, except I knew at all times what my target was not. It was not any of us there in that kitchen on that day. The reality is that I did not have a target. Today, I teach handgun safety. Four of my five sons and my wife all teach handgun safety. From the time of shooting the dryer until now my family continues to provide constant reminders of my mistake.

My sons made up a song to the tune of *I Shot the Sheriff,* but of course it is "*I shot the dryer, but not the washing machine...*" When I have to live through the retelling, which is at almost every family gathering I get to hear comments like, "I can't believe they let you teach firearm safety!"

The fourth general rule is to **keep our finger outside of the trigger guard until we are ready to shoot.** We teach that not only should we keep our finger outside of the trigger guard until we are ready to shoot, but that means more than just our finger. I am not in a position to know what happened with Mr. Webber. My suspicion is that not only was his rifle loaded, but in taking it out of the vehicle it was snagged on something inside of the trigger guard. It is enough to know for this application, obeying all of the safety rules is our personal best protection, and the best protection for those around us.

From here we leap forward in time to a morning in late February of 2011, and again to Redding, California. One of the worst things I can possibly imagine happened when the great grandson of John Stepp, three-year-old Grady Stepp, picked up and pointed a 9mm Makarov handgun, pulling the trigger. He shot through his own brain, living for five weeks in critical condition before being upgraded to fair and stable near the end of March.

The senior Mr. Stepp had a habit of securing his pistol when he got up in the morning. This particular morning, with family plans and everyone showing up earlier than originally anticipated, he simply forgot. The handgun was left in a camera bag, unsecured.

Without further comment on the situations just described, we look at the possibilities of how the state of Oregon could view some of these child endangerment incidents as an emphasis on the need for responsible carrying of concealed or open carry handguns.

If a concealed handgun license holder recklessly engaged in conduct which created a substantial risk of serious physical injury to another person then that person upon a finding of "guilt" in the criminal arena would be held to the liabilities of a Class A misdemeanor. Those liabilities include time in jail and/or fines.

The more knowledge one has, the higher their standard will be raised with respect to their culpability, and we think the more likely they would be found "guilty" of a major crime. For example, a person who merely owned a gun and had no training would be less likely to be found guilty of the crime of Recklessly Endangering Another[17] than a person who had training as an instructor (such as I), had taken a concealed carry class, had a military background, etc.

Onto the particular tapestry of this law we review some facts. In the spring of 2009, then President Dennis Crowell of the Cottage Grove-Eugene Sportsmen's Club took a handgun to the Club. While he attended the Club Board Meeting he left the handgun out where it could be found, and it was found. The person finding the handgun was a 12-year-old son of an attorney in Eugene. That child gave the loaded handgun to another older minor sitting there who knew something about handguns.

A citizen's complaint was filed with the Lane County sheriff's office. They refused to investigate. A follow-up complaint was filed with the District Attorney who was either a member of the Club, or recently had been a member of the Club. Through him his office refused to take any action saying that unless the person complained of was willing to admit to the facts, they would not prosecute.

Based on that response yet another follow-up complaint was filed with the sheriff's office showing the president of the club had made a public apology for his error, essentially admitting the facts necessary for the DA's office to prosecute. The substance of the follow-up response from the sheriff was that since the DA's office would not prosecute, they, the sheriff's office, still would not investigate.

For emphasis: The interesting part is that the facts made known to both the DA and Sheriff included the admission of President Crowell to the Club he had carried the gun into the building. He had put the loaded handgun where it could be, probably would be, and was found by the 12-year-old. His position seemed to be it was the child's fault for finding the gun.

For whatever the real reason, and we have no way of knowing what that was, both the then Sheriff and DA refused their responsibility and duties of their respective offices. The reason for this short story is not to beat up the president of the Cottage Grove-Eugene Sportsmen's Club, the DA, nor the Sheriff. It is to point out that we individually have to be ever vigilant and willing to take the offense in protecting our children from ourselves and from others. That comes from insistence on safe practices, and when we see unsafe practices we do something about it.

In reported news stories through the AP it was noted a three-year-old toddler shot himself to death with his father's gun. March 2012. A young girl died when a sibling fired a gun found in the family car. March 2012. A school girl was seriously wounded when a gun carried in a boy's backpack went off. 2012.

These tragic accidents happened in the span of just weeks in the state of Washington. They have of course raised questions about the effectiveness of the state's gun laws and the community's awareness of firearm safety. They add fuel to the fires of those opposed to handguns in any form (at least opposed to handguns for law-abiding citizens). This is especially true when these types of accidents involve children.

I repeat from the above: In the most recent of these cited situations the child's parent stopped for gas. The father who had a concealed handgun license put his pistol under his seat and got out to pump gas while another adult person went inside the convenience part of the service station. The young boy scrambled out of his child seat finding the gun, which the police say was left in the car by his father. He fatally shot himself in the head.

This followed the shooting death of the seven-year-old daughter of a Marysville police officer, when a sibling found a gun and fired it while the parents were out of their car.

Just a short time before that shooting was the school incident in Washington where a nine-year-old boy was putting his backpack on a desk. The gun inside of the backpack fired critically wounding an eight-year-old girl.

We start closing the loop of this portion of the discussion by going back to the concept of carrying a concealed gun in a vehicle. It is currently a given that with an Oregon concealed license a person not only can carry a gun in a vehicle upon the highways and byways of Oregon, but they can carry the handgun loaded.

I offer a factual consideration: You are driving down the highway/byways of Oregon with a loaded handgun in the vehicle. It is concealed in the console between the driver and passenger seats. You have younger youth in the vehicle. By the nature of the "carry" the handgun is deemed by law to be accessible to all passengers in the vehicle. Now we revisit the laws concerning "child endangerment" as discussed earlier. It is our strongest recommended practice that if you carry in a vehicle with children in the vehicle, make sure the handgun is in your actual possession and NOT available to the children.

In the latest report of the above incident involving one of the Washington children while drafting this portion of the book, the investigation is centering on the concepts of child endangering and manslaughter.

It is a given that most responsible gun owners licensed to carry concealed firearm(s) with them do just that, keep it with them. It is under their sole control. It is where their children cannot possibly get to it without the willing cooperation of the owner.

What I and the news media cannot figure is why these people, one being a policeman, would leave their gun in the vehicle or any other place a child can get to it. Having said that, not everyone can afford a gun safe for storage of their firearms and ammunition. It follows that if they are responsible then they have other ways they can utilize to make their firearms safe, and they will use those before allowing a child (or another adult for that matter) to endanger themselves or others.

Not because child gun accidents make bad press; not because we don't want to deal with the potential legislative negatives and fallout; but because culturally, nationally, and within our team here at Oregon Concealed Co. we value all life so highly, especially that of the innocents, we want to do what we can to educate others for reduction in these kinds of accidents.

We believe those who believe the fallacy that laws protect lives have a myopic view, distorted, and unhinged reality that flies in the face of natural law. Write a law on a piece of paper. Put it on the table. Lay a gun on a table. In the eons of time both will decay to its sub atomic parts without injury to anyone if left alone. When either is in the hands of criminals we, the law-abiding are at risk. It is by the usage and machinations of man they become tools for our destruction.

We advocate for individual responsibility. Parents, make your children safe by education and training. Keep tools of potential personal destruction out of their hands until they have been properly trained and are ready for them.

CHAPTER 5

Travel

S ince the inception of laws designed for vehicle travel as we understand it today, Oregon has applied an "accessibility" standard to the driver and any passengers in the vehicle. The substance of the standard creates a strong presumption that if a handgun is in a vehicle it is accessible to all of those in the vehicle. The public policy driving this standard is the fact that bad guy perpetrators in most vehicular shootings got the gun from the glove box and/or the console or similar holding area in the traveling compartment of the vehicle. The handgun was loaded, accessible, and used. We all want our enforcement/police to have a reasonable amount of ability to protect themselves and to be protected. The outflow from these basic concepts are the vehicle gun laws we have today concerning general travel on the highways and byways of Oregon.

Like so many things, "highways and byways" has a meaning broader than one might commonly think. Some common sense applications are in order. We know the highways, whether interstate, intrastate, or the back roads in the counties such as Pandora are highways and byways of the state. Those federal lands with roadways open to the public such as BLM, the U.S. Forest Service lands for which the feds claim ownership, national parks, and national game refuges are generally considered highways and byways as well.

The part where there is some confusion surrounds roadways across private lands, places like the parking lots at Walmart-type box stores, other private stores, driveways, and Indian reservation lands. This book is not a legal treatise nor is it intended to be a law review article so in keeping it simple, those areas generally open to the public are considered a part of the highways and byways systems in Oregon regardless of whether the owners are public or private.

The 1953 Ford

During the early to mid 1990s there were those like Pastor Paul Revere of the Kingdom of Heaven Church in Sublimity, Oregon who advocated constitutional principles of fundamental rights as they interpreted and understood those rights. One is a right to travel found in U.S. Supreme Court rulings and otherwise supported in basic U.S. Constitutional language. That right was and still is believed by many to include unrestricted right to travel without papers and documentation.

The following picture of such a license is representative and typical of those who carried them. Mr. Seekins is NOT the Mr. Smith referred to below. I represented Mr. Seekins in many cases which could be a book by itself. It is enough to say that when we eventually approached negotiations with the state of Oregon, Mr. Seekins had over 480 citations concerning his insistence on exercising his interpretation of his constitutional principles.

Steve Seekins

Mr. Smith, approximately 35 years old, did not have a driver's license, or at least one that was considered legal. He did have a driver's license issued to him by the Kingdom of Heaven Church in Sublimity, Oregon through Pastor Paul Revere similar to the license above. Mr. Smith lived in the county of Pandora, the city of Somewhere. Mr. Smith was often the driver of a superb black and white, fully restored 1953 Ford with extra loud coreless pipes. Due to his failure to carry a traditional right-of-passage card in the form of an Oregon Driver's License he had been stopped many times, cited, and occasionally arrested. Mr. Smith was well-known to the local city police. So were his car and the sound of it.

On October 3, what was believed to be Mr. Smith's car was heard by the police. They attempted to give chase after hearing the direction they believed Mr. Smith's car was heading, which was to the place where he had returned to live with his parents.

By the time the police arrived at the residence of his elderly parents, if Mr. Smith had been driving, he was out of the car and had walked to the front door. The police came to a screeching halt in the short driveway as Mr. Smith and his brother were entering the house. Both Mr. Smith and Brother flipped the City of Somewhere police the bird, and ran the last couple of steps into the house.

Mr. Smith, in part due to his long experience with the police in advocating his civil rights, knew that if the police had any cause to do anything, whatever it was or could be it would be nothing more than a "violation." In Oregon a violation is not a crime within the criminal code and therefore no part of a violation allows exercising "exigent circumstances" authority to trespass. The police had the duty at that point in time to get a warrant to enter the property because nothing Mr. Smith could allegedly have done would be arrestable. That is if they could even get such a warrant. The ultimate truth of the matter is that there was no probable cause for such a warrant.

This may be hard to believe, but the police, without probable cause that a crime had been committed entered the home by kicking the door in. As they passed by the father who was trying to get out of his easy chair where Father had been watching a football game, one of the officers cuffed Father in the face with the back of his hand. Another one commenting,

"Stay out of this old man." Senior Mrs. Smith was coming out of the kitchen with some tea she had just brewed for senior Father Smith. Another officer pointed a gun at her, telling her, "Keep out of this."

Misters Smith, both John and Brother were found in one of the back closets hiding. Both had guns on their hips, which had not been seen on them as they entered the shared residence.

Other than a little bashing about by the police in making the arrest of the "resisters," dragging them out of the house with one of the police using a "hair" hold on the younger of the two Mr. Smiths, Brother, nothing more happened until they were out on the lawn.

A senior police officer was a neighbor to the Smith family. He knew them all as both friends and good neighbors. He also had been watching TV, in fact the same football game Father Smith had been watching. He heard the backup call on his scanner, quickly dressed in his uniform, and got over to the Smiths home in time to see his comrades drag the two sons out of the house.

After his initial inquiry with other neighbors who were watching and listening from across the street and the neighbors on the other side of the Smiths, Senior Officer told his fellow officers, "You can't do this. You don't have a crime."

The lead officer said, "They had guns!"

Senior Officer looked shocked, "So WHAT!" He practically screamed at them, "They were in their own home!"

About the charges arising out of the pistol/revolver my clients had on their hips—the only real crimes alleged in the arrest—I motioned in the initial case for a pretrial evidence hearing noticing the court that after our success on the motions I would be filing motions for the criminal charges to be dismissed for failure to state sufficient facts to support the City's criminal claims. The court set the motion for hearing.

After the case was dismissed I filed civil lawsuits for trespass, wrongful entry, assault, false arrest, false imprisonment, criminal felony trespass in a civil context (i.e. with guns), etc.

Of importance to this chapter was the ruling on one of the motions I made in this civil case concerning uncontroverted and uncontested facts. I had asked the court to take judicial notice the police were trespassing with their initial stop in the driveway of my clients. The court in its written memo in support of it dismissing this portion of my request noted that the driveway was NOT gated. It was not otherwise secured from public entry. The court further noted the driveway was hooked to the public highways and byways, and that the police had and have as much right to be there as anyone else until demand was put upon them to leave the private property. The court noted that no such demand had been made. The court further noted there were no "No Trespassing" signs or other "common methods" of informing the general public and therefore the police the driveway portion of the property was intended or meant to be secure from general entry by the public.

The trial court went on to say that it was not until the officer or officers kicked in the door was there a possibility of the trespass alleged, etc. As with all of these types of cases we had to get through the initial rounds of motions before the case was postured to settle. I won some of the motions, lost some, but we were headed to trial. The City of Somewhere did settle with each of my clients, the four Smiths getting various amounts of money for the multiple wrongs done them.

Generally, a handgun in Oregon is considered loaded when there is a live cartridge in, or attached to the handgun. There are those who would argue that if the cartridge is in a "magazine" or "clip" as some wrongfully call the ammunition holder, those cartridges are not "attached" to the handgun but rather the cartridge is attached to the magazine or clip. Oregon's position is clear in its governing statute (ORS 166.360(3))—go to www.oregonconcealedlaw.com—that if the magazine with cartridges in it is attached to the handgun in the manner for such attachment, then the cartridge is in the handgun and the handgun is "loaded" within the meaning of Oregon laws.

Next, it is important to understand what it means in Oregon to have the handgun "accessible." In *John and Jane's Fight* above, the handgun was in the passenger compartment of the car. It was not locked in either the glove box or the console. Jane knew it was there. If a person is in (or with a motorcycle "on") a motor vehicle and they DO NOT have a concealed license and a handgun is accessible to them, and they know it is there, then they are in violation of the Oregon concealed carry laws.

Over the years there have been a number of legislative clarifications in the laws and some clarification has also come from the courts.

For the purposes of determining the handgun is NOT "accessible" when one does not have a concealed license the handgun has to be locked if it is in the passenger compartment, or on or attached to a motorcycle. "Locked" as it is used here means that whether the glove box, the console, or the bags on a motorcycle, these areas have to be secured in such a way as to keep the gun from being readily available and accessible to people without an Oregon concealed handgun license who are in or on the vehicle. This is accomplished with a keyed device to unlock the holding area of the console, glove box, or bags.

The legislature went on to address a collateral issue. What if there is no compartment that the handgun can be locked in? For the purposes of ATVs and motorcycles it is enough the handgun is equipped with a trigger lock or other locking mechanism that prevents the discharge of the firearm and that such device is locked without the key in it.

From passage of the initial ATV[18] law in 2009 forward in time it has been repeatedly reported to us by students in our concealed handgun classes that the state police were advising people on ATVs they could not carry the handgun with a magazine, "clip," or with ammunition loose in the same container on the ATV or their person. Notwithstanding that bad advice, the Oregon 2011 legislature addressed this area of confusion for concealed handgun license holders and for clarity for others who do not have a handgun license.

A direct reading of the new statute shows that if the unlicensed person is on a motorcycle or ATV they can have a handgun with them. As mentioned above, it has to be both unloaded and locked so that it is not accessible.

The new statute provides new consistency in the law as well. If a person is an Oregon concealed license holder then they are excused from the strict standard, and can carry their handgun both concealed and loaded. Whether on a motorcycle, ATV, in a car or other vehicle it seems clear it is the intent of the Oregon Legislature that those of us who are law-abiding and have Oregon concealed handgun licenses can have the ability to readily defend ourselves.

The real caveat here is the difference in the standard for what is and what is NOT a loaded handgun. For the general purposes of transportation of ourselves, a "loaded" handgun is any handgun having live cartridges in the gun. However for the purposes of ATVs an "unloaded" handgun is one that if the firearm is a revolver there is no live cartridge in the chamber, that is aligned with the hammer of the revolver; if the firearm is a muzzle-loading firearm, that the firearm is not capped or primed; or if the firearm is other than a revolver or a muzzle-loading firearm, that there is no live cartridge in the chamber.[19]

To more fully understand the approach in Oregon concerning ATVs and off-road vehicles we turn to the statute, which describes ATVs broader than we otherwise commonly understand. ATVs to include. They are those "vehicles" designed for, or capable of cross-country travel, on or immediately over land, water, sand, snow, ice, marsh, swampland, or other natural terrain, and is actually being operated off a highway, or is being operated on a highway for agricultural purposes.[20]

This means that when one is off-roading in a Jeep, SUV, boat, etc., it is unlawful for the handgun to be loaded if one does not have an Oregon concealed carry license.

The exception to the vehicle restrictions, whether on or off road, is when the recreational vehicle or vessel is being used for whatever period of time as residential quarters.[21]

This treatment begs a question of fact: The recreational vehicle, a boat or vessel in this instance (like a house boat) is being towed down the road. In it is a passenger with a concealed handgun on their person. The handgun is loaded with a cartridge in the chamber, ready to fire. The passenger is using the house boat as their residential quarters. What would be the treatment by the law in this circumstance?

The Oregon Court of Appeal found in a comparable situation the "residence" qualified for the statutory exception, that the person was not unlawfully carrying concealed in his truck that was his home.22 What was not addressed was the actual traveling component, but in reading the case the reasoning of the courts would apply, so that in our facts above the persons carrying concealed without a license would be a statutorily authorized carry in their residence.

We close this short section pointing out the irony built into both the statutes and case law with respect to vehicles in general. As we see elsewhere in this book, public places generally are those considered accessible to the public. Most of us would logically and naturally believe that does not include our vehicle. However, in 2008 the courts went so far as to say your vehicle is not a place but rather it is a container. They reasoned it follows jurisdictions authorized to restrict the carry of handguns (and long guns for that matter) can restrict how one is allowed to carry (absent a concealed license), such as a few of the jurisdictions in the Portland area have.

We leave you with the dichotomy of the person traveling in their home going down the highway carrying concealed. We believe the recent treatment of the courts shows us that if the vehicle/vessel is our home/residence while traveling, then the application of ORS 166.250(1) outlining the crime of carrying concealed is trumped by ORS 166.250(2) (B) (b). However, we encourage you to obtain the services of an attorney licensed to practice law in Oregon if you want or need clarification of any portion of this discussion.

We suggest a competent attorney licensed to practice law in Oregon is one who when he or she gives you bad advice, you can sue them, and have a resource called the Oregon State Professional Liability Fund where you can collect the remedies awarded you for the bad advice.

To and From the Gun Range

There is a common misunderstanding concerning the application of the statute allowing the transportation of a concealed gun to and from a gun range. I became acutely aware of this misunderstanding when John Smith came into my office for a consultation and ultimately, representation.

John was traveling from a gun range generally open to the public, but which also had, and has, membership options. With a specific membership a person can use the range and the facilities at all hours. Otherwise, persons like John who are not a members are limited to certain days and certain hours of use. During sighting-in days just before hunting season they have to pay a special fee, which John had done and for which he had a receipt. John sighted in his hunting rifle and generally practiced with his side arm.

In a routine stop for excessive speed he was asked the protocol question by the officer, "Do you have any guns or weapons." John was surprised by the question because the rifle was in a cab rack over the back window. John, like so many of us who are generally law-abiding and basically good people said "Yes." He was then asked where it was. He looked first at the rifle, and then said pointing at the passenger seat, "Under the seat."

"Do you have a license to carry concealed?"

John was surprised, "Uh, no."

The officer asked him to get out of the pick-up and stand by the front bumper. The officer retrieved the handgun, a Smith & Wesson .357 mag. long barrel. They talked a little about why the gun was there, what was going on. John explained that he had been to the range and was coming home. He admitted to speeding, noting that it was a nice day but getting late, and he just wasn't paying attention to the speed.

He was arrested for an illegal carry of a concealed handgun.

Our defense was focused on two elements of the crime. First, the gun wasn't concealed because John had no intention of concealing it. The second defense was pursuant to ORS 166.260(3) (a) which is an exception to the "crime" of carrying concealed. For the exception, that statute says it is not a concealment crime if a member of a club or organization, for the purpose of practicing shooting at targets upon the established target ranges, whether public or private, while such members are using any of the firearms referred to in the concealment crime statute (ORS 166.250) are going to and from the range.

In the pretrial phase the DA and I submitted our anticipated jury instructions based on the facts, most of which had already been agreed to. I was caught off guard when the DA took the position John was not a member of any club or organization. In fact, he had to pay to shoot that day and had a receipt for it.

I argued that because the club was open to the public, the public was its membership. I also in the alternative argued that for the purposes of the applicable statute, payment of the fee bought a "membership" for the day.

The DA argued that for sighting-in-days John had to pay to sight in his rifle.

I argued the crime charged was for carrying the pistol concealed, not the rifle. For the pistol he did not pay a fee and the range was open to him, in fact he had been shooting it on the pistol portion of the range that day.

The judge said he would take it under advisement.

His clerk set a time for us to come back. When I showed up in the courtroom later that week I was directed instead to the judge's chambers. The Assistant DA arrived at about the same time.

The judge told us this was a matter that should be settled and he was willing to *help* us. Been there, done that before. I knew what he really meant, as did the Assistant DA.

The judge discussed the court cases supporting the facts each of us had used as in our arguments of the case law. This was before *State v. Honzel*,[23] a 2001 case that might have given cause for different considerations. He went on to tell each of us we would be other than satisfied if he had to make a ruling and explained how the two rulings would be different. It was clear that with the judge mediating the "negotiation" he would have the hammer if he did not like how either side were conducting themselves, or if our respective clients were being, in his view, unreasonable.

The case ended with a plea of guilty to a speeding ticket.

The 2001 *Honzel* case is instructive. Honzel was stopped for a speeding violation. Honzel had a fanny pack with ammunition the officer somehow spotted. The officer asked him if he had a gun with him. Honzel said that he did and the officer asked if he, the officer, could hold it to be secure during the stop. The handgun was not visible in the fanny pack. After the officer ascertained Honzel did not have a "concealed weapons permit" (language of the court), he was asked why he had the gun.

The trial court noted during the motions phase that Honzel was not a member of the gun club. That was rectified at trial when Honzel presented as evidence his membership card.

Honzel's response was "[I] left earlier in the evening to go shooting at the gun range at Delta Park and before [I] got there [I] stopped at a friend's house." From there he went to where he works in Vancouver, Washington and by the time he was done at his work place, the gun range had closed, so he came home.

The court said:

> "The words "going to and from such ranges" or "returning from" in these statutes have ordinary meanings that are commonly understood. For purposes of this case, they describe conduct that has its beginning point at a statutorily

designated place of activity (the hunting or fishing grounds, or the target range.) Unfortunately for defendant, the conduct permitted by ORS 166.260(2) (a) — going from the target range with a weapon concealed upon his person — never occurred. The fact that defendant intended to go to and depart from the target range when he left his residence with a concealed handgun and the asserted "reasonableness" of his conduct is of no consequence to his responsibility under the statute. Once he decided to possess a handgun that was concealed on his person at a time when he was not going to or coming from the target range, he lost the protection afforded to him by statute."

We are certainly guided by this application of the law by the Court of Appeal. We suggest the language and application of the court is compelling and you should be guided by it also.

This discussion leaves one unanswered question. If you are going to a range on public ground such as BLM or U.S. Forest Service, or a private range that does not require or have memberships, then are you afforded the protection of the statute?

While it is our thought you are a member of the public, and are licensed to carry concealed so for you it will not matter, it is your passenger(s) for which we have a concern. We suggest other parts of this book adequately address this issue without getting into the legal aspects. However, we again advise you to seek independent counsel if this is a concern to you.

In this chapter we have learned:

*   In Oregon a handgun is generally loaded when it has any cartridges in it.
*   It is generally unlawful to carry a handgun loaded and/or concealed on the highways and byways of Oregon unless one has an Oregon concealed handgun license.
*   This includes not only the highways and byways, but parking lots, and driveways generally open to the public.

- If a person expects to keep his or her driveway private, it must be properly posted or secured so as to give notice of the intent to keep it private.
- A person commits the offense of operating an all-terrain vehicle while carrying a firearm if the person operates any snowmobile or all-terrain vehicle (ATV) with a firearm in the possession of the person, unless the firearm is unloaded.
- There are exceptions for ATVs.
- Handguns are not loaded; when the firearm is a revolver, when there is no live cartridge in the chamber that is aligned with the hammer of the revolver; or
- When the firearm is a muzzle-loading firearm, when the firearm is not capped or primed; or
- If the firearm is other than a revolver or a muzzle-loading firearm, when there is no live cartridge in the chamber.
- There are exceptions for Oregon concealed licensed persons carrying on an ATV. Persons so licensed can carry both concealed and loaded whether on their person or the vehicle.

Another exception to when a handgun is concealed is when one is carrying to and from a gun range:

- The range needs to be one designed or used for handguns.
- A person has to have a membership in the range.
- The person must be traveling to and/or from the pistol range.

Competent attorneys:

- A competent attorney licensed to practice law in Oregon is one who when he or she gives you bad advice, you can sue them and have a resource called the Oregon State Professional Liability Fund, where you can collect the remedies awarded you for the bad advice.

CHAPTER 6

The Stop

A good friend called inviting me to go shooting at a local range. In keeping with Mantra #3 (practice, practice, practice) and to visit with an old friend, I was excited about the opportunity. As I was re-cleaning all my pistols and revolvers I received a call.

"Dad, it's Terra (my daughter). Whatcha doing?"

"Nothing honey. Just cleaning guns."

"Ouoo. That sounds like fun." With the tone of voice I could see her grinning.

"Yea, I guess. Watching some *Survivor* as well. Relaxing."

In my mind's eye I could see her eyes twinkle. Girls call their mothers to "girl talk." They call their fathers because they want something. She is married, has a son, a good job, a car, and buying her own home. We are past her getting my vehicle or a twenty dollar bill. "What can I do for you?"

"Well..." The pause was significant. "Johnny (the grandson) is with a friend tomorrow. I was going to take Mom out and was wondering if you would like to do some manly things with John (the husband)." She had her sweet voice on. "It will give you a chance to do some bonding."

It was my turn to pause, but just for a moment. "Put him on." With the commitment to go shooting already in place, I didn't really know if that was something John would like to do but it turned out it was and we finished making the essential arrangements.

Just a little bit about son-in-laws: None of them are good enough for our daughters. That is probably enough said about that.

Just a little bit about John: He was raised different than me or how I raised my sons. His view points are sometimes radically different. John has taught me patience and provided an opportunity for me to come to a new, deeper understanding of myself. In that it has been good. But what makes it work even better is the love he has for my daughter and grandson.

At this time Linda and I were living with my mother, trying to take care of her. (She is more than a little independent.) Mother had survived lung cancer surgery, chemo, and two aneurism surgeries. The chemo took out her kidneys. She has had three fistula surgeries, almost lost her hand from a botched job, and was going to yet another fistula surgery. Dialysis was and is three days a week, four hours a day on the machine.

So to say that I had put things in place for this range time perhaps means a little more than it would have two years earlier.

To compound these matters, I have O.F.S., Old Fart Syndrome. That is where we like to be heard and appreciated, but are getting old enough that we can't do as much, and forget what we are saying.

With the stage set and ready to go, I was out of the driveway when I got a call from my wife Linda. She had taken my mother into dialysis so I thought the call might be important and took it even though I did not have the Bluetooth hooked up.

"Honey, I just called to tell you to play nice with the boys."

Right, like I needed THAT call. I rounded the corner as I laid the phone down, now one and a half blocks from the house. I did not even have time to accelerate when the blue and red lights came on behind me. Worse upon worse. I had pulled up right in front of my #2 son's house with his children, some of my grandkids were in the yard, watching.

The NRA has a lot of "rules" but they are not law. They are best practices derived from long experience. I followed one of them. After pulling over I put my hands at the 11:00 o'clock position on the steering wheel.

The Cottage Grove officer came up to the driver's side cautiously, perhaps more so than I had experienced in the past. He was young.

"Do you know why I stopped you?"

I hoped he had not seen me with the phone to my ear. "I think so."

He pointed with his left hand. "Your seat belt." Sure enough, it was not hooked. I was about to get a ticket and it was my wife's fault! I decided then and there I was really going to give her a piece of my mind about her lack of consideration for my worries about my mother, while she had my mother at dialysis! Right. As Jeff Foxworthy would say, "and the fight was on."

"Driver's license and registration, please," interrupted my calculating thoughts.

In a reflective and thoughtful moment about Oregon's handgun laws I remembered that as a matter of law I did not have to give the officer any information but per the NRA recommendations it might be a good idea. "Officer can we talk just a bit about this?" I actually saw him in my mirror becoming more wary, turning more sideways, and putting his right hand on the butt of his gun.

I don't know if it helped or made matters worse but on the other side of my 1991 beat-up, black Jeep Wrangler was one of my little grandchildren in my son's yard announcing to the others, "Grandpa is going to jail!"

The officer's voice dropped a little. With a slight nod he said, "Yes."

"Officer, I have a concealed license and am armed."

His nostrils flared just a little as he let his breath out. "Oh, is that all. Just put it on the seat." He pointed with his left hand to the empty passenger seat. I am sure he meant the handgun.

I tried not to sound like I was whining. "Can we talk just a little more?"

"Yes."

So in explanation I said, "Well, I am going to the range so I have more than one gun."

He kind of smiled. "Yea, I like to shoot. I understand. Just put them both over there."

"Well, you see, I have one in the shoulder holster." (It was my Glock 19 9mm.)

He nodded. "That is not a problem..."

I didn't give him time to say more. "I have one in my left pocket (a NAA .22 5 shot revolver), and one in my right pocket (a Ruger LCP .380). There is one in the small of my back (a Tarus .357 7 shot revolver), one in the ankle holster (a Ruger LCR 5 shot laser site 38 Special), and three under the seat (Kimber Custom II .45; 9mm Lady Smith & Wesson; Browning Buck Mark .22).

The look of surprise crossing his face tugged at me for yet more explanation. "I am taking my son-in-law shooting. This is all new to him. I kind of wanted to impress him and let him know at the same time he has to treat my daughter right!" I smiled, hoping it did not look as sickly as I was feeling.

The officer looked through my Jeep to the five grandchildren standing behind the fence watching. All were somber, the youngest with tears in her eyes. The officer started to grin. "Well, what is your name?" He took my driver's license without any of the other usual "stuff" and went back to his car to run it.

I saw him in the mirror coming back. He was laughing. I had never seen that happen before, or heard about it, so the immediate thought was that this could really be good. He was in good humor. When he got to my window he said, "Well Mr. Leach. I am just going to give you a warning this time. Next time, if there is one, I will throw the book at you." He looked at the kids.

I know I looked puzzled. As he turned back to me he went on. "Your story has already given me a lot of entertainment today." He leaned a little forward, dropping his voice just a little, "And it will give me more tonight," the pause was longer, "at the doughnut shop." He actually laughed as he turned to go back to his police car.

That is Cottage Grove, Oregon. Less than a week later I was on the bypass in Springfield, Oregon. I am old enough that I watched it being built. From then until even now I have always traveled the average speed everyone else does. Even so, again I experienced the blue and red lights with the first question, "Do you know why I stopped you?"

I said nothing about guns, having a permit, or any other thing related to guns or concealed licensing. What is interesting is that neither did the officer. It was one of the fastest stops, which included the writing of the ticket I have ever had or heard of.

The initial lesson that can be taken from these experiences is that the NRA general advice through those who teach the NRA Basic Pistol Class is good. As we have already learned from above, we get to help set the tone for the general stop.

Our understanding can be expanded. First, the "stop" as we use it here means when and where first contact with the officer happens. To address this with a deeper understanding it is important to also understand the real role of enforcement officers. It is seldom, even less than seldom, an officer is on the scene at the time of the incident that brings him or her there. For those who are actually young enough and/or naïve enough to believe in the concept of "to protect and serve" as a reality of the "now" have not lived in the modern real world very long. I guess that is why we call them "young people."

Today when the police are called for a burglary or theft, the dispatcher will ask the location of the incident. If the location is not politically important to the police, then they follow up with asking the value of the items stolen. Unless the value of the items stolen is significant, boosting the theft into a category of statistical conduct supporting the police in their enforcement efforts, the caller will be told one of a few things.

The first is that they, the police, do not have the manpower due to underfunding to investigate minor crimes. In Oregon if it involves a jurisdiction covered by the sheriff's office, then the caller might be told the matter is civil, especially if there is any way they can justify coloring the facts in any way to show it is civil.

I was called two days ago (at the time this is written in first draft) by a student here in Lane County (NOT Pandora). Her almost new pick-up truck that she had gotten a great deal on was stolen. There was a balance of $500 owed on the truck. She had the title and Bill of Sale. The $500 was owed to the seller of the truck but he had given over the title and Bill of Sale to her at the time of purchase, in part because she had paid so much cash for it.

She was selling the truck and advertised it on Craig's List. Her plan was that when she sold it she was going to pay the $500 she owed and pocket the difference for her other goals and purposes. A third party pretending an interest in the Craig's List listing came out to view the truck. He started it, and then drove away in the now stolen vehicle.

When she complained to the sheriff's office, they asked, "Was anyone hurt?" When she said "no," she was told it was a civil matter because she owed money on the truck. Go figure.

The DA's office refused any kind of action saying that the issue had appropriately been reported to the sheriff's office and it was their jurisdiction. Right!

So, a little about the DA's office. I complained of a gun that was patently left in a condition whereby it could be found by a youth, a form of child abuse/endangerment if it were found by a child and upon conviction. It was found by a youth, a 12-year-old boy. It was loaded. I reported it to the sheriff's office. They said they would do nothing unless there was actual proof of the matters complained of. There was. The person leaving the gun out where it could be found apologized to the Club's board.

The DA's office refused any form of action. I later found out the DA had been a member of the Club although I don't know if he was at the time of the complaint and have not looked it up.

What this repeated short segment teaches and shows is that there is a real world out there, that it has about it elements some would consider corruption, others merely political. Others would have no bad purpose charged to either the Sheriff's Office or to the DA but charge these types of happenings to financial limitations.

The Sheriff's Office in my complaint asked, "Was anyone hurt?" I have thought about and pondered this situation often. Why does the "protect and serve" sheriff's office have to wait until someone is injured? I still don't have an answer for that except to understand some of the fiscal limitations they operate under. For me it is a given they are underfunded. They have limited staff. Further, with a DA's Office that will not prosecute, they are additionally challenged. Added to that is a judiciary that is underfunded, and understaffed.

We are not making a plea here for further funding. I am just noting that in the real world there are practical realities applicable to the situations we may find ourselves involved with. Here in Lane County the current sheriff is hard working and dedicated to the standard of "to protect and serve." However, he too is hamstrung by the lack of funding necessary to run his office with efficiency. He too has to make what are sometimes hard choices.

A perception of my truth, after substantial practice before judges throughout the state, is that many of them get their start by being a political appointee. That means that they have paid their kissing ass dues. What it does not mean is that they have any special level of judicial understanding or judicial integrity.

Another part of the personal perception of truth is that many judges who cannot cut it as attorneys look for the easy way out. They get other people to fund their election opportunity, most often running unopposed when they are incumbents. With no special abilities, or even any real competency, they look for a way out of the general practice of law, and the related hassle of running a business. And after all, who wouldn't enjoy the job of being a judge, whether initially politically appointed or later elected?

It is into this morass of judicial incompetency, underfunding, and understaffing we are thrown when we as honest and law-abiding citizens get a license to carry a concealed handgun. We should not expect, and if we are prudent we will not expect, any justifiable balance between the various branches of government designed to protect us from government in the course of exercising those rights guaranteed to us by the federal and State of Oregon constitutions.

This circular discussion brings us back to what is the function of the enforcement officer? If the officer is a true Executive Branch person, i.e., a State, County, or City police officer, then he or she is the designated first responder for gathering evidence at the scene of the event or crime. The burden falls on him or her to do a good job of observation, inquiry, and reporting. It is culturally our expectation that in doing so they will be impartial and forthright. They have a duty to record all of the relevant information concerning the event. If you or I are the object of the investigation, they also have a duty to record any exculpatory comments or statements we might make. Exculpatory means statements that show we didn't do whatever was claimed, or in the alternative we were justified in doing what we did.

All of this brings us back to the "stop" in whatever form it might take. It makes the officer's job easy when the bad guy admits to not only being a bad guy, but in the particular circumstances of the stop, the bad guy admits to doing the wrongful acts with an intent to do the wrongful act.

"Did you John Smith carry your gun concealed?" It seems straight-forward enough as far as general questions go. So Mr. Smith is going through the trauma of the stop. He has not read this book or other material from other organizations that support the carrying of concealed handguns, especially in Oregon. Because the handgun could not initially be seen by the officer he assumes it was concealed.

The facts may be substantially different but he doesn't think about all of those. So Mr. Smith responds, "Well, yes, I did."

Or if the question is presented differently, like, "Why Mr. Smith were you carrying your handgun concealed."

Mr. Smith responds to either of the questions with some excuse. In this case he says, "Well, I thought the brush might dislodge it from my holster."

In the first question Mr. Smith has directly admitted he was carrying the handgun concealed. In the second question he has inferentially admitted he was carrying the gun concealed. With either of those answers the enforcement investigator's question is now going to be aimed at Mr. Smith as if he were the bad guy because he has admitted he is the bad guy.

Road Rage

A good friend of mine, Bill Smith, who had taken his Oregon Concealed Handgun License Class from me, was going south on the I-5 freeway in the right hand lane. With a big truck on his immediate left, an 18-wheeler ahead of him, and a small white car right behind him, he was boxed from moving over to make more room for the freeway on-ramp as a much older car was trying to enter the mainstream of traffic. That car had almost caught up to Bill on his right, trying to merge into the freeway traffic. At a crucial decision-making juncture the driver of the old car sped up but was unable to find a spot to join traffic. He had to almost come to a stop as he neared the end of the merge lane, but managed to pull in behind the small white car.

Bill told me he noted how difficult it was for the old car, and noted to me that if the guy had simply decreased speed a little he would have gotten in behind the white car without difficulty or the almost emergency panic stop gyrations that started near the end of the on-ramp.

The next thing Bill noticed was the old car had not only sped up passing the little white car using the left lane, but it was beside him on his left. The guy in the old car "looked scruffy with an unkempt beard and a cigarette in his right hand." While Bill was glancing at him, the visibly angry man reached out with his right hand and flipped Bill the bird, dropping his cigarette on the passenger seat.

In doing so, he swerved to the right for just a moment, not much. Bill in turn swerved to make sure there was no contact at freeway speeds. Bill's level of angst went up when the guy deliberately swerved again at Bill. Bill said that he could see the guy clearly. The guy who is now "Bad Guy" not only appeared angry, Bad Guy was mouthing the words "fucker" and "son-of-a-bitch" which were obviously directed at Bill, and again with the hand gestures.

Bill slowed a little.

Bad Guy slowed a little.

Bill sped up.

Bad Guy sped up.

Bad Guy again swerved at Bill, getting closer this time. Bill again swerved to his right, over the fog line this time.

Bill started to slow down and Bad Guy started slowing down yet again. Bill stomped on it, putting the peddle down hard on the otherwise somewhat gutless Xterra, gaining enough quicker speed to pull ahead of Bad Guy, and into the left lane to pass the next truck, another 18-wheeler. When Bill passed on the left he made sure he left no space for Bad Guy to slip around during the pass. Bill was past the long truck, and after pulling again into the right hand lane he hoped Bad Guy would just pass him this time. But Bad Guy did not. Instead, when Bad Guy got up beside Bill again, he again swerved. This time it was so aggressive and drastic a swerve that Bad Guy crossed the center line, into Bill's lane.

Bill said his "*Oh Shit!*" factor went way up. His Smith and Wesson .357 magnum was under the seat. His Ruger LCP .380 was in the console. He pulled the Ruger out with his right hand and put it up in the window where Bad Guy could see it. Bill said he remembered a portion of the class and was not going to, and did not point his handgun at Bad Guy. He just showed Bad Guy that he had it.

Bad Guy did see it and started to slow down, but then sped up, passing Bill without any further incident. Bill slowed down just a little to put even more distance between them as he put the small five-shot pistol back into the console.

After Bill settled down just a little, he regained enough presence of mind to call 911. Dispatch asked Bill to stop at the next exit where the police would soon arrive to take his report. What Bill did not know was that Bad Guy had already called 911, reporting his version of the incident.

Life became substantially different than what the police dispatch said it would be. Bill was arrested for "pointing a gun at another." I got the call to come get him out of jail. Of course in the process his pistols were confiscated. His Xterra was impounded, and they took his concealed license.

During the course of the stop and arrest the police kept trying to get Bill to admit he 1) pointed the gun at Bad Guy, 2) did so out of anger, and 3) with careless disregard. There is much more to the stop, including Bill's PTSD and responses under stress. *What Bill did not do was admit to any of those things!*

Having pounded Bill with poor jokes and law school witticisms, Bill wisely did as outlined. At what turned out to be the stop he admitted nothing, denied everything, and counter charged.

One of the wiser things Bill did when questioned closely was when he said, "I feared for my life and the lives of others around me on the freeway who could have been hurt if there were a high speed wreck." He repeatedly asked the sheriff's deputy why they didn't get the other guy. He told them over and over the Bad Guy was the problem. And he said he was only acting in self-defense, showing that while his gun wasn't as big as the Bad Guy's vehicle, he did have a way to defend himself. Bill repeated the standard, "I feared for my life!"

Bad Guy was from another state, Washington. While the police initially would not disclose the Bad Guy's name, they did say he was just passing through on his way to southern California. I was sure Bad Guy did not intend to come back to testify.

Ultimately this ended with the DA dropping the charges, and Bill getting his guns and concealed license back. Of course there was not a mechanism for Bill to be reimbursed for the impounded vehicle he had to buy out of hock or the rolling impacts on his PTSD.

Some of the lessons we have already learned from other stories above and pearls again shared in this story are:

- Be the first to call 911;
- Don't show the gun unless you intend to use it;
- Comply with the instructions of the officers;
- Use the magic language, *I feared for my life*;
- Use the magic language, *I want an attorney*;
- Admit nothing unless compelled;
- Deny everything if compelled;
- Counter charge (if it can be done without admitting anything).

Golden Lips – Being the "Good Guy"

Ron is a real property appraiser. He has worked at appraising land and houses for almost 40 years. One of his clients, the state of Oregon, often uses his services as do local Universities and other "notables." His driving record was and is clean. Sometimes when the appraiser boys get together on Thursday mornings, he gets a gentle ribbing with someone asking him if he had a ticket yet. It seemed that he had the golden lips, having always made a favorable impression on the police the few times he had been stopped, saying just the right things and driving away with only a warning. Usually that warning was verbal. I think this is because Ron is at his core law-abiding and honest. Those traits show through in his words and actions.

So the phone call came as a surprise. "Don, you will not believe what happened. I just got out of jail. You can't believe what happened." Repeating himself like that sounded like he was in shock. The pause was long.

"What happened Ron?"

"Well, you know the interchange, getting on the freeway in Somewhere?"

"Yes?" I tried not to sound too curious.

"I was getting on there to go out to.... Can you represent me?"

"Ron, you know the health issues I have and that I sent in my bar resignation." I explained how difficult it would be for me to get my license reinstated and how long it would take. I ended with, "With all of this the timing is wrong and costs are too prohibitive for just one case. Besides, I don't even know if I physically could do it."

Ron explained he was going down the road when he was pulled over by a state of Oregon police officer shortly after he started accelerating on the on-ramp to I-5 South. He was stopped initially for failing to yield.

Ron told me, "I had a lot on my mind, it was just an oversight and I did yield. I just took a little longer to do it. Ya know, if I actually failed to yield there would have been an accident."

"Well Ron, maybe that is why the officer stopped you."

In other circumstances he would have been grinning. I could envision that rueful smile in my mind's eye when he said, "Dah, ya think?" Next he asked, "So what is going to happen?"

"Tell me more of the story."

The Story

After pulling Ron over, the officer did the typical and routine cop stop thing. "Driver's license, registration, and insurance card please."

As Ron was reaching for the glove box he remembered that he had put his pistol in there after being to the range just a few days before. He had forgotten the little .22 Beretta was in the glove box until he was actually reaching for the registration and insurance card. The side note is that from where the officer was standing the officer could not see into the glove box and Ron's vehicle registration and insurance card were clipped to the edge where Ron could easily to get to them.

Ron stopped. "Officer sir. I just remembered. I have my little pistol I took to the range the other day in there."

Ron admitted to me that he was *just trying to be helpful*, to keep from having an issue.

The nature of the stop changed, with the officer becoming more aggressive, and even more businesslike. He asked Ron a lot of questions about the gun ending with, "Let me see your concealed license."

Of course that was not going to happen, "I am sorry sir, but I don't have one."

The rest of the stop was by the numbers, with Ron standing at a modified form of attention, hands spread on the hood of the SUV.

I suggested to Ron that maybe he was coming back from the shooting range, and therefore was privileged to carry the pistol in the glove box.

"I can't say that. It would be lying. Besides, I already told the officer that was several days ago." Ron went on to rationalize the DA wouldn't do anything because he, Ron, was a law-abiding citizen, never had even a traffic ticket (although he had come close a few times), always paid an honest tax, and lived within the boundaries generally imposed by society through the social compact and laws.

"Ron, you are too good to be true. The DA is going to eat you alive. I think I will change your first name to 'Statistic.' That is what you are about to become."

Ron had survived Vietnam with no physical scars. When he came stateside he put all of that behind, treating it like it was, a bad nightmare. With his past behind him, even though he was soon to be 60 years of age, Ron, like so many people, was naïve with almost a third grade sense of fairness. His true world according to his belief system was one where only bad guys are arrested. Only bad guys go to jail.

During the discussion I told Ron how I thought it would all go down, that the DA would see him as a statistical furtherance of the DA's political goals and purposes. I suggested that even though the DA could treat the charge as a violation which is non-criminal, instead of the charged crime of a misdemeanor, the DA would not go there. I suggested having a loaded pistol in the glove box would further weigh in the view of the police who would as a result put some pressure on the DA for misdemeanor treatment.

Ron believed he could "just talk to the DA" and it would all go away.

"Ron, what could possibly make you believe that? Get your attorney to do the talking."

The real answer of course lay in his mistaken belief that the system was designed to protect him, the good guy.

Ron became a criminal in the Oregon system with a sentence of thirty days in jail (served on weekends), community service (150 hours), fines, and a record. Jail time was suspended subject to Ron's successful community service and fine. He was told his success in meeting his court ordered obligations would cause the matter to be treated as a successful diversion.

With the successful completion of his "diversion," even as I write he is now exploring his record to insure this matter is not causing him to be listed as having a criminal record. Now of course he wishes he had obtained an attorney on the front end of this matter instead of the back end.

There are some things we have already talked about which need to be reviewed again, adding to our new uderstandings:

- The trial starts when the lights go on.
- The COP is NOT your friend.
- The DA is not your friend.
- Your attorney is not your friend (but the best you can do under the circumstances).

CHAPTER 7

Trespass in Oregon

Castle Treatment in Oregon – Curtilage

In the first level of discussion about the castle doctrine in Oregon we look at what comprises the "castle" or home as it is more commonly referred to.

Curtilage is the immediate, enclosed area surrounding a house or dwelling. The U.S. Supreme Court noted in a case called *United States v. Dunn*, 480 U.S. 294 (1987), that curtilage is the area immediately surrounding a residence that "harbors the intimate activity associated with the sanctity of a man's home and the privacies of life.'' Curtilage, like a house, is protected under the Fourth Amendment from "unreasonable searches and seizures.'' The Fourth Amendment is designed to protect us from unlawful intrusions of government.

The basic concept is that not only is your privacy in your home a sanctity you are unquestionably allowed to protect, if the immediate area surrounding your house is defined in a way to let all know you intend it to be a portion of your "castle" or home, it too can be such. The next issue is how does one set up that area so that it can be a part of the "home?"

The bottom line is that determining the boundaries of curtilage is imprecise and subject to controversy. Four of the factors used by courts (from the above referred case) to determine whether to classify the area as curtilage include:

1) The distance from the home to the place claimed to be curtilage (the closer the home is, the more likely to be curtilage);

2) Whether the area claimed to be curtilage is included within an enclosure surrounding the home;

3) The nature of use to which the area is put (if it is the site of domestic activities, it is more likely to be a part of the curtilage); and

4) The steps taken by the resident to protect the area from observation by people passing by (shielding from public view will favor finding the portion is curtilage).[24]

March 7, 2011 in Portland, Oregon

Whether as a would-be robber or a man simply wanting a shower, Timothy Chapek, 24, after breaking into the home of Hilary Mackenzie barricaded himself in her bathroom and then called 911 for a rescue. She had unexpectedly arrived home about 7:00 p.m. and caught him by surprise. Poor Timmy was worried that Hilary might be armed (or that her barking German Shepherds could prove problematic).

In his 911 call seeking help he told the police operator, "I just broke into a house and the owner came home."

"You broke into a house?" the surprised operator responded.

"I think she's got guns," Chapek added.

Almost simultaneously, Mackenzie called the police to report that there was an intruder in her Portland home (she told an operator that Chapek had reported he was taking a shower). The pair's dueling 911 calls can be listened to.[25]

Chapek told the police that he just wanted to take "a shower, nothing more."

Mackenzie asked, "Why are you in my house taking a shower?"

Chapek responded, "I broke in. I was kidnapped."

He told her his name. When Mackenzie tells Chapek that she's calling the police, he says, "I've already called them. They're on the phone right now."

Chapek told the police that a group of men had kidnapped him and put him in the bathroom.

Mackenzie and her daughter had returned home from running an errand at the grocery store Monday night when they heard a man's voice coming from their first floor bathroom.

The bathroom windows were fogged up and a towel was thrown over the stall of the shower. Chapek still had a wet head from his shower.

Mackenzie, in her own call to 911, said that her daughter first thought there was an intruder.

"My daughter said 'I hear a man in the house,' I thought, oh no, don't be silly," she told the 911 operator.

Mackenzie reported that none of her belongings were out of place and that Chapek had "earlier made some utterance...that 'Mexicans' had kidnapped him and put him in the bathroom."

Chapek was arrested and charged with criminal trespass.

In this story no one is claiming Chapek was or is the brightest person ever arrested. But the important part of this story is not what happened to him or the circumstances surrounding his entry into Hilary Mackenzie's home. It was his fear she *might* have a gun that prompted him to call 911 for rescue. Whether her home or curtilage she had a fundamental and constitutional right to expect privacy and security.

We further explore what curtilage is to understand the foundational terms for when our right to justified self-defense is triggered by a burglary, arson, or other possible criminal trespass under the law. In the constitutional sense and the Fourth Amendment we are protected from intrusions into our privacy by enforcement (government) without exigent circumstances (chasing a person believed to be a felon) or a warrant provided we have made clear our intention to be free from intrusions. In the home that concept is already clearly understood in the common law. A person's home is their castle. But what about the area outside of the home? To understand that potential limitation we continue to look at the actual application of the law by the courts in *Dunn* above.

Generally we find curtilage includes the common law understanding of what curtilage is, which is a family use, a domestic use, and associated with the domestic nature of a home use. The actual language of one of the cases[26] in quoting yet other cases say as again outlined from above, "At common law, the curtilage is the area to which extends the intimate activity associated with the 'sanctity of a man's home and the privacies of life,' and therefore has been considered part of the home itself for Fourth Amendment purposes."

That court goes on to say, "A person who wishes to preserve a constitutionally protected privacy interest in land outside the curtilage must manifest an intention to exclude the public by erecting barriers to entry, such as fences, or by posting signs." They go on to say this intention has to be clear.[27]

What flows from this short second prong of the discussion is that there are three views of our property. First there is the castle, our home. Second is a domestic use area we have protected under the outline above, the curtilage which gets the same treatment as the home when properly and appropriately designated. Third, there is that which we have defined by posting signs and barriers as our general property to be kept "private." That which is not our castle and not domestic use (curtilage), but otherwise so defined as our private property with a higher expectation of privacy.

The reason this distinction is labored here again is because most defensive shooting happen from within our castles or upon the curtilage surrounding it. It makes a difference in how the law will look at the factual circumstances when we are NOT inside the house but still on our property. Are we within the curtilage (still our castle) or merely with a higher expectation of privacy from trespassers?

The answer to this question can make the difference between a pat on the back and prison.

For the uninitiated they are now confused. When can I shoot? The answer goes back to discussing the use of "justification" above, the use of responsive deadly force (*see* Chapter 2).

The self-defense justification standard, which defines when it is allowed in defense of self or third parties where the person using a justified forceful response is using it to protect him or herself from the wrongful unlawful use of force or other force intended, or likely to produce, death or serious bodily injury. The deadly force being used for protection can only be used for as long as is necessary to eliminate the unlawful use of force likely to produce death or serious bodily injury.[28]

The difference is we are now discussing when in the defensive shooter's castle he or she may be entitled to some presumptions. If the unauthorized bad guy person or persons have crossed that threshold to invade the castle then BGs are there for serious wrongful acts. It is an allowable presumption that if the defensive shooter said they feared for their life, they did. As with all presumptions, it can be overcome by the facts as judged by any of those who can lawfully judge that situation.

When the person is lawfully in possession of what we call the "subject property" but outside of the home and curtilage area, they do not have that same level of presumption. The unlawful use of force by the trespasser will be tested by a more objective standard with no allowance for the sanctity of the home/castle.

Warning: As with all such standards, they will be tested by the factual circumstances of the situation.

Our recommendation is that where practical each person should establish the domestic use of their real property by definition, which at a minimum would include a gated fenced area and the **proper posting of signs as outlined in Oregon statutes.**

I know this without a doubt, if I were a defensive shooter with BG kicking down the fence to my curtilage I would have a much better chance in the Oregon system of laws than if as a defensive shooter BG was kicking down the fence over two miles from the main house on the perimeter of the 17,000 acre ranch (that I actually once owned).

In Oregon, regardless of the higher presumption concerning curtilage, the defensive shooter still has to be able to say, "I feared for my life (or the life of another in his or her presence)," and only engage the defensive deadly force posture for as long as the BG is unlawfully using force intended or likely to cause death or serious bodily harm.

As a cautionary note, I use "intended or likely to cause death or serious bodily harm" to assist in understanding the actual language of "justification" within the Oregon statutes.

We emphasize a second time from a direction differing in light of the reoccurring, but conflicting, message we get from other states with make-my-day laws, which are also called "castle" doctrines. In a make-my-day state there is a presumption the Bad Guys are in fact Bad Guys by the operational fact they are wrongfully in the "castle" of the defensive shooter. Thus, the defensive shooter is what we call in Oregon, "justified" as a matter of law. That is NOT the castle law in Oregon.

In Oregon a person is NOT justified in using a deadly physical force against another person unless the defensive shooter reasonably believes the Bad Guy is committing or attempting to commit a felony involving the use or threatened imminent use of physical force against a person; or the Bad Guy is committing or attempting to commit a burglary in a dwelling; or the Bad Guy is using or about to use unlawful deadly physical force against the defensive shooter or a third party in the presence of the defensive shooter; or last, BG is using unlawful force that can cause serious injury.

Federal Limitations Concerning Handguns

This federal list is not exhaustive and not intended to fully outline the basics of carrying a handgun concealed on or in those places jurisdictionally reserved to federal governance. Nor is this list intended to be legal advice. Within the context outlined in this book, we request the reader to more fully explore the alternatives when considering carrying a concealed handgun in a federal reserve or jurisdiction.

We are discussing where a person generally *cannot* carry a handgun, concealed or otherwise. When listing federal courthouses it is with the understanding that the limitation discussed is for the purpose of a "carry" whether concealed or otherwise. There are exceptions for police officers, federal agents, etc. The burden you and I operate under, due to these general restrictions, include parking lots adjacent to or part of the facility if the federal agency/entity owns or has control of the parking lot or a particular portion of the lot has been reserved to the federal agency/entity. If it only controls a portion of the parking lot, then the restrictive prohibition applies to that portion under the control of the feds.

We do not engage whether a "federal building" is a legal building properly authorized under federal and state of Oregon laws from the viewpoint of the extreme political right. It is enough for the purposes of this book to say we are discussing the general concepts and applications of the law as they are understood and applied at the time of this writing. So "building" as it is used here includes those building or portions of a building claimed to be owned, leased, or rented by the federal government and/or its sub-parts.

Of special note are buildings within the real property reservations of the federal government such as Bureau of Land Management and the United States Forest Service. Each of these units of government have their own Code of Federal Regulations (CFRs). Whether BLM (43 CFR) or USFS (36 CFR), there is no federal law prohibiting a "carry" in the National Forests or on BLM grounds. The alternative view is provided by rule which states in substance the laws of the state governing the state grounds will apply to the federal holdings as well. It follows that if the state, Oregon in this instance, allows the carrying of concealed handguns by license, then one so licensed can carry on the said federal grounds. Oregon does allow the carrying of concealed handguns by license.

Other limitations on carrying concealed or even carrying at all include federal prisons, U.S. Army Corp of Engineers projects, national cemeteries, generally military bases, Amtrak, post offices, and Indian reservations (Note: Reservations are controlled by Tribal Law. If you have more interest than this surface treatment, those laws can be looked up on the internet for each tribe).

To ensure public safety and for the protection of public resources the following gun related acts are generally prohibited on those lands generally considered public lands.[29]

- Discharging or using firearms or fireworks in a developed recreation site (campgrounds and day use areas).
- Willfully damaging or destroying property, structures or resources (including but not limited to signs and trees).
- Creating a hazard or nuisance (shooting from or across public roads and trails and/or in any manner endangering the public).
- Possession of an unregistered assault weapon as defined by the state laws you are in and DOJ regulations.
- Littering (please pickup and pack out all targets, expended shells and other personal trash).
- Hunting in violation of applicable state and federal laws and regulations.

Those with concealed carry handgun licenses can carry their personal protection firearm concealed while sojourning in national parks and wildlife
refuges. However, consistent with the general view of the federal government, weapons will not be allowed in buildings where federal employees
work, such as the Statute of Liberty, or Washington Monument. But restau-
rants, hotels and gift shops will be subject to the new[30] gun laws so the
lawful carrying public can carry concealed in those portions of their buildings. Yosemite's historic Ahwahnee Hotel, for example, must allow visi-
tors who are legally entitled to carry concealed handguns to bring them
into the building.

An interesting side note is the fact federal employees, except those specifically designated to perform enforcement, police, or other official duties requiring the use of firearms, are prohibited from carrying, or having in their
possession, firearms on property under the control of the BLM Secretary. Employees who are officially stationed in parks, refuges, Indian reservations, other Tribal lands or other wilderness areas which are known to be inhabited by
wild animals are permitted when on those lands to carry and use firearms for
personal protection. That carry has to be permitted by existing policy or as
authorized by the park, refuge, or area supervisor. Notwithstanding this para-
graph, employees who are not on official duty may carry firearms on Depart-
mental lands under the same conditions and in accordance with procedures
and authorizations established for members of the general public.[31]

One of the more notable places to carry reserved to federal officers
and certain police are airports.[32] However, not only are you and I denied
the right to carry to defend ourselves past the security screening in airports,
we have a typical report from November 23, 2010
(www.dailymail.co.uk/news/article-1332307/Now-abused-TSA-staff-vent-
anger-security-patdown-searches.html) worthy of review that talks about
the abuses of the TSA.

As the luck of life happens, shortly after preparing the above I ran into an
old acquaintance I prefer to consider a friend. He is an officer of the law that
for these purposes I will simply call "Officer." In other jurisdictions I had sued
him, along with other officers, the city, and the county several times. He now
works as a federal enforcement officer on Veterans' Administration adminis-
tered grounds and at their facilities.

We spent some time talking about his views and approach to handguns at the VA hospitals and outreach building in Oregon. In order to have this discussion I had to agree that I understood these were his personal views.

When Officer has to deal with a firearms situation, the first protocol is to control the situation, to take control of the firearm which usually means taking control of the perpetrator. Just a couple of days ago he had to intervene when a Vietnam veteran who was going to see a shrink insisted on taking his rifle with him. The veteran knew he was unsafe without personal protection and used the example at Fort Hood where the bad guy, a member of the armed forces, killed 13 and wounded 21 others.

After taking control of the situation and weapon, Officer develops a case file, and at the least writes up a report.

State Limitations: This book is focused on Oregon and those limitations are related individually throughout.

CHAPTER 8

Other Issues

M ost of this work has been kept in simple language, generally staying away from quoting statutes, administrative rules, or case law. Part of the purpose has been to aid the reader who is NOT an attorney or trained in the law to more easily understand the thrust of the presented material. Another part has been to reduce the reading material so that this book is a manageable size. With that said, not everything written by the legislature or the courts is necessarily complex or convoluted in such a way as to render it by its very presentation confusing.

There are many definitions of what a public building is within the laws of Oregon. The controlling definition would be the one found in Title 16, Chapter 166[33] that governs the laws concerning concealed handguns.

We have already learned and it is worth repeating here; public buildings are hospitals, the capitol building, schools, public and private, including colleges and universities, city halls, and the residences of elected state officials. This type of view includes the grounds adjacent to these buildings. Who would have thought that your neighbor you elected to an "at large" position, who has a house and surrounding property, have properties considered to be "public" within the meaning of the statute? The entertaining thought is trying having a picnic on his or her lawn and see what happens or to go on a sight-seeing visit to the "Public Property" of the house. But I digress.

By the definition "public building" extends even further in that "portions" of building that are occupied by an agency of the state or municipal corporations are also considered for these purposes to be public buildings.

Open Carry

Oregonians in discussion of their rights with me have often held out with pride the fact that Oregon is an "open carry" state. They understand they have the right to openly carry a firearm/handgun. Most recognize that to do so means the firearm is openly displayed. It is not uncommon to hear them say they can openly carry and then see them slap their hip.

This is NOT fully consistent with the applicable statute[34] outlining illegal concealed carry which states, "Firearms carried openly in belt holsters are not concealed within the meaning of this section." For example, an openly visible shoulder holster with a handgun technically is NOT a "belt holster." We could drive this factual application further but we believe the simple treatment outlined above is sufficient. In summary, if it is not concealed, hidden from view with the purpose of having it hidden, then it will most probably be treated by the courts in Oregon as other than concealed. We advise you to seek legal counsel if you have a specific situation for which you need advice.

Even with the easily understandable outline above, Oregon laws allow incorporated localities to restrict the open carrying of loaded firearms for those who do not have a concealed handgun license.

- "Open Carry" means to carry the handgun in plain view in a belted hip holster.

Sheep Skin Coat

Early in my practice in Salem, before I had a secretary, and being brand new to the practice of law, a potential client walked into my office. "Mr. Leach?" I looked up from my less than six-month-old desk.

I was surprised because I didn't hear him come in. As I looked up, "Yes?" His story unfolded. John, 47 years old, owned the family ranch and logging business. He was a fifth generation from pioneer stock in Pandora county on the Southern Oregon border. With his brother, a friend, and a couple of hired hands they had been rounding up cattle from off the government (BLM) grazing allotment. From daylight it had been a long, cool, and generally blustery day. It had sprinkled a little rain off and on, but they had not really gotten "wet."

To John it had been a big help to have the long sheepskin-lined riding coat designed for wearing while riding horses. That is a coat that is a little longer so it will cover the crotch in the front and is split in the back as well so it will lie over the horse for the rider's comfort while he is in the saddle. The design also helps keep him more fully covered when he is not on the horse. With the leather chaps and well-greased cowboy riding boots, a western attired horseman is reasonably well-protected from the elements. This particular day passed into afternoon.

No cowboy worth his salt would pass up coffee at the lunch break but whether he or the cook forgot, coffee was not to be found. The trip into the "town" of Somewhere was short, at least relatively short for people who live "out."

At the local Safeway store he never gave a thought about how he might look to strangers otherwise passing through town. "Stranger" called the police reporting a menacing person with a fumanchu mustache, wild look in his eyes, carrying a gun hidden under his coat was in the store. Stranger reported that he left the store rather than being a part of what was sure to become a bad scene "with the obviously outlaw nature of the gunman."

Of course the city police arrived. Mr. Smith was at the checkout having just paid for the coffee. He had picked up a "treat" of chocolate for one of the hired hands who liked it in his coffee. Somewhere Town is one of the larger towns in Southern Oregon so it is common for the younger local police to not know everybody. Notwithstanding the checkout clerk had just said, "Fun to see you John, see you next trip" as she waved, the officers approached. They stopped John before he could get out the door. Just as a quick side note, the clerk was a third cousin to John.

The discussion that followed flowed down the slippery slope of mutual misunderstandings before voices started being raised in anger. Backup arrived for the cops. The new arrivals of course did not see or hear any of what went on before. What they had was a report of a man with a gun and a backup request. What they saw was a big man looking rough and dirty. He had some kind of cowboy Stetson hat pulled down a little low over the eyes. The stained, sheepskin coat and chaps that looked like they could walk by themselves were not reassuring. The well-worn cowboy boots looked like they were Goodwill rejects. His voice was deep and angry.

Mr. Smith may have crossed the invisible line when in response to the next question he said, "Piss off. I'm going back to the ranch."

Officer 3 or 4, from one of the two backup cars that came in late noticed the bottom of the holster sticking out beneath the stained coat. Catching everyone off guard, the officer drew his gun, pointing it at Mr. Smith. "He's got a gun. He's got a gun!" Other officers drew their guns. All of course were pointed at Mr. Smith.

They ordered him to turn around, and then the routine. After they had taken his gun, an old Colt .45 revolver, they tried to decide what to actually arrest him for. One of them suggested they take Mr. Smith down to the jail and decide there, which is exactly what they did.

A part of the decision-making process included a call to the DA's office. Three of the officers admitted to the DA they could see the holster. None of the officers could actually see the gun, but they collectively ruled out the concealed weapon charges noting that they had enough visibility of the holster that any reasonable person who saw it would conclude he had a handgun and therefore was not carrying concealed.

Having already functionally arrested him, they decided there was something in the matter that was arrestable. They used an argument that he was "constructively" arrested when they did the "stop" and questioning. It was the position of the city DA he had attempted an "escape" when he tried to walk away before the questioning had been completed.

Of course there were many holes in this type of analysis but the DA was really building a case for immunity for all of the officer actors leaving only the City to answer the counter charges for civil rights violations.

I took a $500 dollar retainer. The DA strung things out further and further. A second retainer.

Where Mr. Smith and I started from was his strong statement that fighting the misdemeanor charge was a matter of principles. "I don't care how much it costs, I will see this through!" With the third retainer Mr. Smith's comments were "If we could just get this trial over, I am ready to move on." All discussions of a civil rights lawsuit had passed. And that tells the end of this story.

Well almost. The prohibition in ORS 166.250 is against carrying a concealed firearm. Enforcement officers generally considered a handgun concealed if it is out of view. The law as we have discussed earlier in this book generally carries with it a "mens re" or element of intent to break the law. However, in the statute it is specifically noted that "firearms carried openly in belt holsters are not concealed within the meaning of this section." ORS 166.250(3).

It follows that we can openly carry in all places we are not specifically restricted from. Those restrictions in Oregon include federal buildings and offices, and some courthouse building. Other courthouse buildings that generally serve the public but have only a portion of the building set aside for the actual courts will only have the court sections closed to handguns. The rest of the building will remain open.

The U.S. Postal Service is generally considered a federal building and one is prohibited from the carry of any firearms in the post office or in the parking areas supporting the post office. In the designated parking areas it is illegal to even have the handgun in your car. So for example we have a Social Security outreach office in a building. It has three designated parking spaces as a part of the lease which are properly signed and lined. It is illegal to park a vehicle in those 3 spaces if the vehicle has guns in it even though you can park next to the lots with no issue concerning handguns.

Whether BLM or U.S. Forest Service, it is illegal to park on the grounds/parking lots supporting those buildings when there are guns in the vehicle. As a practical matter people who go hunting and have need for information and other services from the BLM and USFS often take their vehicles onto those properties with the rifles in the racks of their pickup or other vehicles. Understanding that the buildings and supporting parking areas are treated differently than the broader lands managed by the BLM and USFS, care should be taken when going into any of those buildings.

CHAPTER 9

School Grounds

The issue of concealed firearms in schools and universities in Oregon has been hotly contested for many years. Recently, the issue came to the forefront and received extensive coverage in the press as challenges to policies banning concealed firearms in public universities were litigated in court. In the aftermath Oregon law has on its face been upheld. Those laws state public K-12 schools, colleges, and universities cannot prohibit a properly licensed individual from carrying a concealed handgun on its property. The Oregon Court of Appeals has confirmed this for public colleges and universities, though Oregon courts have yet to weigh in on the issue of concealed handguns being carried by properly licensed individuals on public K-12 school property. The lack of judicial insight into the matter does not mean that public schools in Oregon can ban concealed handguns. For this reason the Oregon legislature has received considerable pressure from various groups to pass legislation allowing local school districts to prevent properly licensed individuals from carrying concealed handguns on school property. The most recent of these attacks came in 2012 with the introduction of Senate Bills 1550, 1551, 1594. So far the legislature has rejected those attempts.

The reason why public school districts, colleges, and universities in Oregon cannot prevent a properly licensed individual from carrying a concealed handgun on public school property is that the Oregon Legislature has not granted the authority to do so to any unit of government. Oregon law, specifically ORS § 166.170, explicitly restricts the ability of any unit of government, except for the Oregon Legislature, from passing any regulation that affects the "sale, acquisition, transfer, ownership, possession, storage, transportation, or use of firearms...."[35] This means that although the Oregon Legislature believes it can prevent a properly licensed individual from carrying a concealed weapon on the property of a K-12 school district, a college, or university, no other unit of state or local government has the authority to do so unless the Legislature decides to grant it such authority in the future.

It is important to note, only properly licensed individuals may by statute carry a concealed handgun on public school (K-12, college, university) property. The Oregon Legislature has explicitly made it a felony to possess a firearm in any public building (including hospitals, the capitol building, any public or private school, a city hall, or the residence of any elected state official) by anyone who does not have a concealed handgun license, or is otherwise authorized to do so by law (such as a police officer).[36] Additionally, federal law prohibits anyone to possess a firearm in a "school-zone," except for individuals properly licensed to carry a concealed handgun and those authorized to do so by law (such as police officers).[37]

Public Universities and Colleges

The Oregon University System, made up of the seven public universities in Oregon, is governed by the State Board of Higher Education.[38] The State Board of Higher Education, as an agency of the State of Oregon, has the authority to adopt rules for the governance of the institutions under its control, including the grounds and buildings of the various public universities.[39] The rules adopted by the State Board of Higher Education have the force of law and must be complied with by both the public universities and anyone interacting with them.[40]

Those rules prorogated by the Oregon University System have the same force and effect as if they had been passed as statutes by the Oregon Legislature when those rules are authorized by and within the scope of statutes, even though such passage is a clear violation of the Oregon Constitutional separation of powers between the Executive, Legislative, and Judicial Branches of Oregon government.

In 1991, the State Board of Higher Education adopted a rule imposing sanctions on individuals who possess or use firearms on university property, including those properly licensed to carry a concealed handgun.[41] The sanctions imposed for a violation of the rule depend on the status of the individual. A student would be sanctioned under the educational institution's student conduct code, an employee would be subject to discipline or dismissal, and a visitor would be asked to leave the premises. If a visitor refused to leave, the institution could press criminal trespass charges against the visitor.

In September 2011, the Oregon Court of Appeals invalidated this rule because it was contrary to ORS § 166.170 (discussed above) reserving the right to make such laws solely and exclusively to the legislature.[42] The Court of Appeals stated that the rule promulgated by the Board of Higher Education was exactly the type of regulation affecting the possession of firearms that the legislature intended to prevent when it passed ORS § 166.170. No governmental unit in Oregon, whether it is at the state or local level, can pass ANY regulation affecting the possession of a firearm without the explicit authority of the Oregon legislature. Additionally, the legislature has explicitly addressed the issue of firearms on college and university campuses and has banned the possession of them while on college or university property.[43] However, the legislature has also explicitly excluded concealed handgun license holders from this law when it was enacted.[44] This lends support to the contention that the legislature did not intend for there to be concealed handgun restrictions imposed on properly licensed individuals. For the same reasons discussed below with respect to public K-12 schools, individual colleges, and universities also cannot pass their own policies restricting the ability of properly licensed individuals from carrying concealed handguns on public college and university property.

Public K-12 Schools

In Oregon, public K-12 educational institutions through their school boards have rulemaking authority granted to it by the Oregon Legislature for the governance of its school[45] and for the use of school buildings for civic and recreational purposes.[46] When a school board passes a policy according to this grant of power by the Oregon Legislature and following the Oregon Administrative Procedures Act, it becomes a rule with the force of law.[47] All students, staff members, and individuals interacting with the school district must abide by these rules or they can be penalized according to whatever sanctions are proscribed by school district policy. Although local school boards have broad general rulemaking authority to create policies that have the force of law, their power is not unlimited. School boards must abide by the United States and Oregon Constitutions, federal and Oregon statutes, and rules adopted by the federal and Oregon Departments of Education. If a local school board policy runs counter to anybody of law with greater authority than it, the policy is illegal and the local school board has exceeded its authority in its rulemaking procedure.

As discussed above, the Oregon legislature is the only governmental entity in the state that can pass any regulation affecting the possession of a firearm. If a local school district has a policy that prohibits a properly licensed individual from carrying a concealed weapon on public school property, that policy is therefore illegal under current Oregon law.

Many public school districts in Oregon have school board policies that ban weapons on school property, including firearms and concealed handguns carried by properly licensed individuals. For example, Portland Public Schools has a policy prohibiting weapons on school district property, and defines weapons to include firearms.[48] The Portland Public Schools policy does not mention concealed handguns carried by properly licensed individuals, and is similar to policies enacted by other school boards in Oregon, including the Willamette Education Service District.[49] Eugene School District 4J has an even more restrictive policy, and explicitly prohibits all weapons on school district property or at school-sponsored activities off school property.[50] The Eugene policy specifically prohibits "concealed weapons permit" holders from possessing a weapon on school property or at an off-site school-sponsored activity.[51] The Eugene School

District 4J policy further states that any person who is not a student or staff member and is found to be in possession of a weapon, including an individual with a concealed handgun license, "will be considered to be unlawfully present on the premises and will be subject to prosecution for criminal trespass in the second degree."[52] On the other end of the spectrum is Springfield School District 19, which, while it does have a policy banning firearms on school property, recognizes that concealed handgun licensees can legally carry a concealed handgun on school property. They, through their policy ask for such properly licensed individuals to voluntarily comply with the school district policy.[53]

Despite the existence of such policies, it is universally understood that currently in the State of Oregon, public schools cannot prevent a properly licensed individual from carrying a concealed handgun on school property and at school-sponsored activities. In nearly every term of the Oregon Legislature, legislation is considered that would grant local school boards with the authority to prohibit properly licensed individuals from carrying concealed handguns on school property. In fact, hearings were held in the Oregon Senate Judiciary Committee on such legislation in May of 2011 and again in February of 2012. In the first instance the bill did not make it out of committee. In the second it did not survive a vote of the Senate.

Additionally, the Oregon School Boards Association (OSBA) has admitted that it is legal in Oregon for a properly licensed individual to carry a concealed handgun on public school property.[54] The OSBA frequently lobbies the legislature to pass legislation that would grant local school districts with the authority to prevent concealed handgun license holders from carrying handguns on school property however their efforts have not yet been successful.

It is important to note that while a school cannot legally prevent a properly licensed individual from carrying a concealed handgun on school property, school districts can enforce other policies that do not deal with possession of a weapon to exclude an individual from school property. A refusal to leave school property in the face of a violation of such a policy could subject an individual to prosecution for criminal trespass. Additionally, as discussed above, possession of a firearm on public school property by an individual without a concealed handgun license could result in felony prosecution under Oregon law as well as prosecution under federal law.

Finally, although a school district cannot prevent a properly licensed individual from carrying a concealed weapon on school property, a school district can prevent a properly licensed employee from carrying a concealed handgun on school property if such a regulation is a part of an official employment policy. The Oregon Court of Appeals has held that the internal employment policy of a public school district does not rise to the level of a universally applicable regulation of firearms that the Oregon Legislature sought to prevent.[55] Because an internal employment policy is not a universally applicable regulation rising to the level of an ordinance regulating firearms, the employment policy of a public school district is not contrary to ORS § 166.170 (discussed above) and a public school district can prevent its properly licensed employees from carrying concealed weapons on school property. This matter is yet to be heard and ruled on by the Oregon Supreme Court.

It is my personal belief such an employment rule is in fact unconstitutional under Oregon Constitution Article I, Section 27 and the statutes outlined above. We further note this issue has not been litigated at the Oregon Supreme Court level in the light of recent federal Supreme Court cases such as *Heller* and *McDonald*. We believe Oregon's highest court will not now support such a ludicrous finding but caution you, the reader. It is the thrust of this book to encourage you, and all concealed handgun license holders to follow the current laws as they are defined, unless you are willing to be the poster child for possible change.

Private Schools: K-12 and Universities

While private schools, including private K-12 educational institutions as well as private colleges and universities, must comply with certain state and federal regulations dealing with areas such as school-year length, teacher qualifications, and compliance with local codes including building, occupancy, health, and fire codes, they are generally free to operate without much interference from the state. Such private educational institutions are not bound by the same constitutional and legal requirements related to concealed handguns as public educational institutions.

Although Oregon law grants properly licensed concealed handgun carriers the right to carry a concealed handgun in public; private schools, just like any other private property owner, are not bound by such requirements. Any private property owner, including a private educational institution, has the right to develop rules and policies that individuals must comply with in order to lawfully enter and remain on the property. Such rules or policies could range from a dress code to a rule prohibiting profanity. If an individual does not comply with the rules or policies of a private property owner, the non-complying individual can be asked to leave the property. If the non-complying individual refuses to leave, he can be arrested and charged with criminal trespass.

A private school, just like a private homeowner, can lawfully ban firearms from its property, including those carried by an individual with a permit to carry a concealed handgun. For example, if Private Elementary School X has a policy prohibiting all weapons, including concealed handguns carried by a properly licensed individual, and it is discovered that an individual is carrying a concealed pistol, School X can ask that individual to leave. If the individual does not leave, he can lawfully be prosecuted for criminal trespass.

Finally, it is important to note that Oregon law does make possession of a firearm in a private school a felony, just as it does for public schools and other public buildings.[56] However, as with public schools and other public buildings, Oregon law explicitly exempts any individual who is properly licensed to carry a concealed handgun from this law.[57] Unlike public schools, a private school can lawfully ban all firearms, including concealed handguns carried by properly licensed individuals if it so chooses and goes through the hoops of proper notifications (signage, notices directly, etc.).

A Note on Criminal Trespass in the Second Degree

In several places above, the possibility of prosecution for criminal trespass in the second degree was discussed. It may prove useful to understand what this means. Criminal trespass in the second degree occurs when a person "enters or remains unlawfully...in or upon premises."[58] In Oregon, it is a Class C Misdemeanor and is punishable by up to 30 days in jail and a fine of up to $1250.[59] Additionally, one can be charged with criminal trespass while in possession of a firearm, which is defined as committing a criminal trespass while in possession of a firearm.[60] In Oregon, this is a Class A Misdemeanor and is punishable by up to 1 year in jail and a fine of up to $6,250. As you can see, a conviction for criminal trespass should not be taken lightly, and these consequences should be considered if you are asked to leave a property, even if you believe you have a right to legally carry a concealed handgun, because you are a properly licensed individual carrying a concealed handgun.

- Oregon departments, agencies, and other political subdivisions are restricted by statute from making laws impacting lawful concealed handgun holders.
- Generally when licensed and carrying concealed in public schools, keep the handgun concealed.
- Do not carry concealed on properly posted private property, even schools. To wrongfully carry on private school grounds can lead to criminal misdemeanor charges.

CHAPTER 10

Don't Ask, Don't Tell, Don't Show – Mantra #1

Casino – Oregon

In our live classes we are often asked about whether a licensed concealed handgun person can lawfully carry concealed in a casino in Oregon. The problem with a direct answer is that each tribal influence would have us believe they are a law unto themselves, outside of Oregon laws.

With that said, again, this book is not intended to be a legal treatise. So I went to several of the closest tribal influences and inquired directly at the following casinos: Three Rivers in Florence, Oregon; The Mill Casino in Lincoln City, Oregon; Seven Feathers in Canyonville, Oregon; and Spirit Mountain. It was a tough duty but someone had to do it.

I talked to the on-shift head of security and one or more security guards on "floor" duty at each casino. Each told me I was the first to inquire in a very long time. In my inquiry I asked how often someone asks whether they can carry concealed. They all said "No one asks." Some were not sure of their actual policies. Some did not know whether their policy, whatever it was or is, is posted. At Three Rivers we had a general discussion before the memory of one of the security officers was triggered. He recalled a posting somewhere, he thought, by the two main entrances.

We proceeded to go out into the foyer and look. There was the posting which I asked to take a picture of with my cell phone camera. They said "Sure."

As our guest we want you to have a winning experience. We only ask that you follow a few rules.

- No one under 21 years of age is permitted in the gaming area.

- Three Rivers Casino has the right to limit one machine per guest.

- It is illegal to cash out or play found credits.

- No outside alcohol is allowed in the gaming area.

- Cameras are not allowed on the gaming floor unless approved by Management.

- Weapons of any type are not allowed in or around the property.

- Electronic communication devices are not allowed at the gaming tables.

Also, federal and tribal laws prohibit the use of our gaming chips ouside our casino for any monetary purpose whatsoever and that these chips are the sole property of Three Rivers Casino.

Gaming is regulated by the Confederated Tribes Gaming Commission. Any gaming issue that can not be resolved by casino management should be brought to the Confederated Tribes Gaming Commission located at:

1845 Highway 126   Florence, OR 97439   541.997.2830

Casino Rules

After going back inside the young man working floor security informed me all the casinos in Oregon had the same requirements.

I was thoughtful. "As many times as I have been here and there," I kind of waived my hand in the direction of North and West, "this is the first time I have read that document. It doesn't seem adequate to me. What do you think?"

He smiled first, then his face took on a more serious look. "Well," the pause was significant. "We don't ask. On the few occasions I have been asked by someone carrying, I tell them to leave it locked in the car. I say, 'if you are carrying, go put it back in the car.' They leave and I assume they did so."

I don't know whether I looked as puzzled as I was feeling. "What do you do then? Do you follow them back out to make sure they put it in the car?"

He looked at the door, thoughtful. "No. Really, I have only had a couple of those potentials. I didn't see the gun so I didn't worry about it."

I asked, "So, we teach in our classes don't ask, don't show, and don't tell. That seems to be what you are saying here. Would that be a fair assessment?"

The head security person for the day inserted himself into the conversation. "No. Everyone has to follow the rules. Everyone."

My problem with this dialogue dates back years to a situation where I represented OSHA. The law surrounding Bureau of Indian Affairs Trust Lands is both convoluted and complex. The "then" application of whether Oregon or Tribal law would apply was not easily answered.

The above posted document in the Oregon environment would lack sufficiency to be enforceable. It has conflicts built-in on the surface, where in the first sentence it talks about "rules." We have no meaningful way to find out if these so called "rules" are in fact "laws" with the full force and impacts of law under the Oregon umbrella of statutory controls. It is further deficient in that it does not provide "reasonable notice" to the general public. It is possible however it is sufficient under Tribal Laws.

I admit my ignorance. I will continue as I have in the past. I will not ask, will not tell, and most certainly will not show. I suggest this is a choice for consideration for each and every law-abiding concealed license holder. I know this, if everyone who carries refused to go to the Indian casinos, that would have a significant impact on their business. It follows logically where the casinos are built for a money-making enterprise the tribal elders would consider carefully the impact(s) of any decision surrounding their treatment of persons otherwise lawfully carrying concealed within their building.

A Gun in Jail

In the mid 1990s I was Chairman of the Riddle School District School Board, on several youth committees for Douglas County, and a practicing attorney. I had read and understood the concealed license requirement in Oregon, specifically with respect to carrying a gun on school grounds. So with my license I had no real concerns and wore my North American Arms boot revolver all the time, concealed. It had become such a habit that I would get up in the morning and after putting my boots on, put the holster and gun in the top of my boot without even thinking about it.

With criminal defendants there was and is a thought within the legal defense community that unless the matter is a felony, it is enough to meet with the defendant just before the trial. I treated every representation as if it were a felony. Thus, I met with every client charged with a crime, sometimes many times before the trial. I had gone to the Douglas County Jail to visit with a court appointed incarcerated person I was representing.

After checking in I made it to the "attorney" room and was soon sitting with my client with only the two of us in there. As we discussed the potential evidentiary issues and what he felt would be his best defense I came to the realization this man was truly a "bad" person as we in an otherwise normal society would think of such things. The following thought was me wondering, "*Just how safe am I?*" That was followed with an immediate thought, "*What if he overpowered me, took my gun, and did bad and dastardly things to me and to others in the jail?*" Realizing that I hadn't even thought of the gun when I checked into to the jail, it seemed it was a little late now.

Looking at my face he asked, "What's wrong?"

I really wanted to meet with my afternoon appointment in Eastern Oregon later that same day so it was important to me to finish the interview and evidence outline. "Nothing, I will be right back." I asked the guard if he could be kept there, I had something to do. With the positive response I went out to the jailer.

I asked her, "Can I leave this here? I forgot I had it." I put the little .22 mag. revolver on the counter separating us. She freaked out, almost off her nut. She put her hands out in front of herself as if warding off the ultimate evil from the dark pits of hell. Her eyes wide, shock on her face, she yelled, "Get that out of here. Get it out of here right now!"

It was only a couple of minutes before the little revolver was hidden in my black 4-wheel drive Jeep Wrangler, soft top. Right! How does one secure a soft top? I locked the Jeep up with the gun where it could not be seen. I went back in to finish my client interview. When I reentered the jail the only thing they did not do was a full cavity search before letting me back in to see my client. I thankfully soon finished the interview.

Next was a quick trip to see the sheriff where I explained exactly what happened and gave my promises and assurances I would not make that mistake again. He actually laughed with me and ended with, "I am sure it won't again. Maybe this was a good reality check for all of us." We shook hands before I left.

I thanked him yet again a little later in writing in a most humbling manner for being so understanding. But for that day I left for my appointment, the Jeep Wrangler full of camping gear to hunt with the boys near East Lake in the Paulina Unit.

A sheriff's lieutenant sent a letter to all attorneys in Oregon, as well as all presiding judges in each of the counties, and each of the city judges (they have a list). Copies of it went to the Federal Ninth Circuit District Judges as well. It told them I had worn a gun not only into the sheriff's office (which was OK), but into the jail (which was NOT OK). The lieutenant noted to do so is a felony and that being an attorney does not excuse anyone from the law. He ended by further noting now that everyone had notice of the sheriff's office official position, if anyone in the future carried a gun into the actual jail portion of the facility they would face felony prosecution.

For the next couple of years when I showed up at court in some other jurisdiction, the judge would invariably ask, "Are you the same Mr. Leach who wore a gun in the Douglas County jail?"

With a bowed head, "Yes your Honor."

"Do you have one now?"

"No your Honor, I do not."

5th Street Market

In about 2004 or 2005 my wife Linda and I were at the Fifth Street Market in Eugene, Oregon. I was and am personally offended by their policies on how one is juried into the outdoor booth opportunities. Generally I do not support them in any way but my wife had indicated a strong interest in going "to see what was going on." We found a number of views displayed that do not match our core beliefs. Even so the experience was entertaining. I worked to keep my conservative mouth shut, my one statement worn on my T-shirt, "Earth First, We'll Log The Other Planets Later."

I was watching people and otherwise enjoying the late summer weather. Linda was at a booth supplying cedar products, from hope chests, to little jewelry chests, and boxes. The craftsman ship was superb. As I turned towards where Linda was standing, I saw a middle-aged man approach another who was obviously his friend. The man that got my attention was excited, talking about his new handgun.

"Well, let's see it," the friend asked.

The man produced it from somewhere. I never gave it a thought as to whether he had a concealed license. It appeared to be something like a Glock or Springfield carry 9mm pistol. As he was talking to his friend I saw others observing the two of them. The facial appearances of those others showed their displeasure. One of the observers had his cell phone out.

"Linda, let's get out of here." I took her elbow to steer her out of the little shop.

She pulled away, "What is your rush?"

I nodded toward the gun toting individual. "I think there is a gun issue brewing here." I nodded again toward the two men oblivious to their surroundings, and the impact they appeared to be having on some of the other people around them.

Probably related to one of Murphy's Laws, the Eugene City police showed up before we actually had time to get out of there. Any other time they would have been late, way late!

"We had a report of people brandishing guns."

That was how in part it started with the man with the gun protesting for his rights. As the confrontational discussion escalated one of the police said they would consider his having a gun and showing it around either as "brandishing or exhibiting" or as a "nuisance." The police threatened an arrest.

Linda and I did not hear the rest of that discussion as we walked away. We didn't get to see the final outcome of the confrontation. What I know is what we believe and preach in our live classes, "Do not ask, tell, or show!" Had the man with the new gun exercised a little discretion he would not have had to deal with the police.

Stolen Gas

In about 2004 I had a thief or thieves stealing gas from my 1991 Jeep Wrangler where we lived on State Street in Salem. The first time I called the Salem Police they told me I had to report it to the County Sheriff because I lived outside of the city limits about 100 feet away. Going toward downtown from my home the next street on our left was the city limits. They were right, we were in the county.

I called the Marion County Sheriff's Department to complain of the theft of my gas. They told me that it was a property crime and not serious enough to come out or to investigate. They told me that they were under-budgeted. The officer emphasized they had to focus on serious crime. That angered me so I asked why they could focus on minor speeding tickets then. They apologized saying they could do nothing more for me re-emphasizing the fact they were underfunded.

I called three more times over the next two months, each time after gas had been stolen. Nothing. They offered no suggestions, no help of any kind.

After pondering, meditation, trying to embrace the "now" of the continued happenings I had an enlightenment. Acting on that moment of insight, after the next theft I put my Glock 17 9mm in my waist band where any who looked could easily see it.

I went down to the street dividing the jurisdictions of the City of Salem and the County of Marion. As people would come to their doors, I could follow their eyes to the gun so easily visible. I had knocked on all of the doors in that neighborhood but two asking, "Does anyone know the little son-of-a-bitch that has been stealing gas from me?" Of course no one did.

Just before I finished, the City of Salem police showed up. (At the time I was on their side of the street too.) They had their little bull horn. "Sir, take the gun out, lay it on the sidewalk, and take three steps back. Carefully."

Of course I did just that.

The one who had gotten out of the car walked up to me carefully, "Just what do you think you are doing?"

"Your job!"

The other officer had come up, also carefully with his hand on his gun but neither had pulled their guns. The first officer reached down, picked up my Glock, took the magazine out and looked to see if I had a round chambered. I did not. Why wasn't it chambered? I don't know, because I almost always carry chambered and ready. In reflective thought maybe it was because I was not really looking for a fight.

The ensuing conversation was frustrating to the officers as I reminded them they and the county sheriff's office were so busy with serious crime they could not investigate the theft of my gas. But they could somehow find the time to come out and hassle a law-abiding attorney citizen who had done and was doing nothing wrong.

They told me to go home, the one officer taking all of the ammunition out of the magazine. He handed me the 17 rounds, and then the magazine. I put the rounds in my pocket with the ammunition. The officers got in their squad car but just sat there waiting to see what was going to happen.

I pulled a full magazine loaded with 9mm fluted hollow point ammunition, the recommended self-defense load, inserting it into the area designed for it. After putting the gun back into my waist band yet again I considered the last two houses. But I had pushed the envelope as much as I felt I could safely, so I started walking back to my house. They followed me for about two blocks before they took off at a slow crawl.

The interesting side note to this is that no one stole any more gas from me.

Summary of Ask, Tell, Show

After the above experiences and dealing with gun issues with clients I developed the "don't ask, don't tell, and don't show" mantras we teach in our live classes and our online class. In retrospect, most situations I and/or my clients faced with enforcement came from violations of one or more of these politically defensive concepts.

Nothing about these mantras is intended to replace common sense. There are times when we do show our guns; we ask others about their guns; and we talk about our guns. The simple truth of this is that we need to make sure of the surrounding environment we are in and be aware of those who we do not know that could mistake our intentions or live in their own worlds of fear.

In the late summer of 2011 I was sitting in the Koffee Kup, a cafe in Cottage Grove, Oregon with a number of friends. The conversation turned to guns and before long we all had our guns on the table talking about the merits and benefits of one gun over another and which caliber could be the best in particular circumstances. No one in the cafe showed any concern at all. Even the two city police officers in the next booth were unconcerned. Before their break was over they had joined us for the conversation.

In looking from there further back in time: I was in my first year of college at the University of Oregon (1966). I had been expounding on the local wisdom of youth gleaned from that hot bed of liberal educational opportunity to my Democrat father. He appeared to be listening. I was at that age when we still know everything about anything even though I was in the process of developing a 1.26 GPA, and "yes," my first run at a higher education ended in new opportunities after I flunked out. We call it "military life."

My father started shaking his finger at me, "Donnie, listen to what you are saying." My father was old-school so for him to actually try to communicate without name calling got my attention.

"Son, no amount of education can compensate for a lack of common sense." So I leave you the reader with this, if you lack common sense, you should not carry a gun. If you have common sense, use it if you need to.

CHAPTER 11

Read, Study, Learn – Mantra #2

I project based on my own experiences: As a responsible person who actually carries a concealed handgun allowed by law and a part of my fundamental constitutional right, it is my hope I never find myself in a situation where I have to defend myself or others. I want a more lawful and safer world. But I have made choices due to my own experiences and my health condition that dictate the necessity of carrying protection from those who would unlawfully use deadly force against me or my loved ones, or otherwise attempt to do us serious bodily harm.

Read, Study, Learn – Knowing the Standards

Some members of the Club wanted to change Club uses. Some of course did not. The ABC Gun Club was in internal political turmoil. At a meeting in November of 2008 one of the members with support of one of the Board of Director ("BD") members proceeded to outline their views of both the "why" and the "how" anticipated changes would be embraced by ABC. They lied.

I had an opportunity to address the issues. In that process I noted that both BD1 and BD2 had "perhaps misstated the truth of the matter." It was with specificity that I pointed out the "inaccuracies" of their statements.

It is common in such situations to see a hardening of the attitudes and polarization of the various political positions. Even so I was surprised at the willingness of the Board of Directors to embrace the lies and what appeared to be deliberate misdirection's of the advocates for change. As it is said, "having been to the rodeo" I understood what was going on. It was their Club and ultimately they would do whatever they had determined in their "behind the scenes politics" to be in their perceptions of what would be their collective best interests.

After the meeting was over and in the presence of other Board of Director members and some of the general membership I was confronted by BD1.

"Are you calling me a liar?" He appeared angry and was definitely threatening in his speech and demeanor. I was immediately lost in thought while trying to keep my attention on him. Wondering how to respond, how to possibly diffuse the situation, I put my right hand on the .380 Ruger LCP in my right front pants pocket. With the health issues I have I knew I was not a candidate for retreat and worried about even the immediate stress of this situation.

"You called me a liar!" This short fat man's mouth was drawn into a thin line as he clearly and deliberately enunciated each word.

"Well, I did say that I thought you misspoke the truth. I guess you can make of that what you will." I had turned partially sideways to him so my crotch would not be as readily exposed. I also knew that even though my hand on my gun would not be visible, it would now be less visible. It was comforting to know the 9mm Glock 19 in the shoulder holster had 16 rounds of fluted hollow point bullets, even though the gun was mounted on my left side for the convenience of a right-handed person such as me. For the uninitiated, the standard Glock 19 magazine holds 15 rounds with the 16th in the chamber. It was chambered as was the .380.

He drew my pondering back to what was happening. "I said you called me a liar." While not louder, he was more intense, a little spittle at the corner of his mouth. I think BD1 was perhaps emboldened by my failure to respond further.

"Well, put so bluntly, I guess I did by inference, but that is not what I said."

He took a small shuffling step forward. "Come outside, right now. We will settle this like men."

That almost made me laugh. It sounded more like third grade playground antics. I said, "I think not."

Mr. Smith arched his back, throwing his blubbery belly into me just a little. "I said, let's go outside and settle this." He again pushed a little with his belly. "Like men!"

A lot was going through my personal filter system. I was thinking about all that I had learned through various readings, the applicable law, and the potential various outcomes. What I knew, what weighed heavily on me was that if I went out there, I was going to a gun fight. I also knew that it was likely in the aftermath of the shooting that was sure to happen, I would have to deal with a "mutual" combat situation and possibly a murder or manslaughter charge.

I could see no way out of this situation other than to save his life which I really did not and do not care about one way or another. So to keep me from the stress that was sure to follow plus being able to keep me out of jail and/or prison I decided to save his life.

"BD1, I am not going out there with you."

He threw his fat belly at me again, hitting me with the Jell-O like blob a little more firmly. He said, "let's go outside. Let's settle it, here, tonight."

I shook my head "no."

"I thought not you cowardly..." He let it stop before he said more. Perhaps he feared that if he pushed me too hard I would go outside. BD1 left with two of the other board members and others of those who would call such a person "friend." It actually was like a playground thing. A couple of others standing close by who heard everything came up to me, commenting how badly they felt about his misdirected stupidity. One of them I had been pistol shooting with that very morning. He knew I was armed.

I waited long enough to insure that if BD1 was outside waiting for me it would NOT be a *mutual combat situation*, regardless of whatever developed from this point in time.

The reason for this true story is to emphasize the importance of knowing the standards for defense of self and others. The bottom line is this, the situation of mutual combat modifies when one can and cannot use a gun in self-defense or defense of another.

We learn these standards by taking classes like those offered by Oregon Concealed Handgun License Classes DBA Oregon Concealed (*OCHLC Co.*, an Oregon Corporation for Oregonians by Oregonians and *Oregon Concealed Co.*, another Oregon Corporation by Oregonians and for Oregonians) which go the extra mile in providing the practical aspects of how to carry responsibly and when one can use self-defense/defense-of-others in their protection. We read books like this one and others of a similar nature.

Oregon Concealed Co. offers their online class for free at www.oregonconcealed.com. We suggest people serious about their personal and family defense take this class periodically. We have had many young adults, old enough to fight and kill on foreign soil, old enough to vote, but not old enough for their concealed handgun license, take this class for the information it provides while they wait for the miraculous intervention of time and maturity so that they can get their license and carry concealed in these threatening times.

We suggest supporting material such as magazines, news spots, and internet articles that provide depth and understanding about our responsibilities when carrying a concealed handgun.

CHAPTER 12

Practice, Practice, Practice – Mantra #3

I am reminded of the situation of Mr. James McCullough published by the Omaha World-Herald April 30, 2010:

> Harry James McCullough, a former security guard was standing at a Walgreens checkout counter when he saw two masked men, one with a sawed-off shotgun, enter the store. Marquail Thomas, 18, pointed the shotgun at customers and yelled, "Nobody (expletive) move!"'
>
> "There's no doubt in my mind what they were going to do," McCullough said. "There was no time to react. You only have one chance."
>
> McCullough pulled out a pistol and shot Thomas four times. Thomas collapsed outside the store and died later at a hospital.
>
> McCullough chased down the second masked man, whom Omaha police have identified as Angelo Douglas,

17, and held him until officers arrived. Jauvier Perkins, 15, who police said was the getaway driver, was arrested Wednesday.

Prosecutors said all three are known gang members.

McCullough said he had no idea whom he was dealing with.

"I took it personal," he said. "I was the only one in that situation that could have made it any better, so I took action."

McCullough said he never expected something like this to happen at his neighborhood drugstore, which he visits at least once a month to pick up a prescription for migraine headaches.

"I didn't have time to be scared," he said. "It happened so quickly. You have to swell up and be bigger than your surroundings. If you portray yourself as big as a bear, you are a bear."

McCullough was not charged in the Monday night shooting. McCullough was cited by police for carrying a concealed weapon.

McCullough said he has had firearms training, shoots guns competitively, and has had security jobs.

"I carry my gun everywhere I go. It's like my wallet," he said. "It's a personal protection and a safety thing."

He has a valid permit to carry a gun in plain view, typically in a holster. Police said he pulled the pistol from his waistband. McCullough said he never applied for a state permit to carry a concealed weapon because it costs "extra money" and he felt that Omaha's carry permit was "sufficient."

He said he's shaky and hasn't been able to eat or sleep much, taking only catnaps. He said the thought of retaliation is "in the back of my mind," so he doesn't stay at one place for a long period of time. However, he said, he isn't going to change his life because of fears about what might happen. He plans to continue to carry a gun if he isn't convicted of a concealed weapons violation.

"I'm not going to sit in a corner and hide," he said. "I'm going to live my life."

He said he has been interested in weapons since he was a child.

McCullough shot Thomas with a .40-caliber pistol. He said that the weapon can hold 15 rounds and that he remembers shooting four times Monday night.

The shotgun Thomas was carrying was unloaded.

Kleine said McCullough fired eight rounds, hitting Thomas four times.

Thomas was shot once in the right hand, once in the left arm, once in the middle of the chest and once in the lower back. Kleine said the wound to the back doesn't mean that McCullough shot Thomas as he was running away. He said the shots could have spun Thomas around.

Kleine said a bullet from the pistol was found inside the barrel of the shotgun, indicating that Thomas was aiming his gun at McCullough.

McCullough said he feels for Thomas's family, calling the shooting "unfortunate." But he felt he had to act.

"To me, he's just a robber in a mask," he said. "I think the city has had enough of the crime."

At OCHLC/Oregon Concealed we teach the other half of the Basic Pistol class, a shooting skills class, as well as Safety and Firearms Familiarity. We have access to several ranges and encourage our students to practice, practice, practice. In the moment of peril, of necessity, those who are prepared for that which they wish they did not have to face will be able to respond with practiced experience improving their opportunity to be successful in the defense of themselves and third parties in their presence. Again, practice, practice, practice!

CHAPTER 13

Citizens' Arrest & The Public Policy

The Arrest

Jane Smith had been attending a series of classes on Citizen Rights at the local Community College, in Pandora County, Oregon. It was an extraordinary and insightful class. The person teaching it with his Doctorate of Laws and in-depth practical experience added much to the Socratic dialog. At the end of each presentation unit he was complimented by the attendees. Those classes covered such topics as children rights, senior citizen rights, administrative law, trespass, citizen's arrest, etc. I add humbly as the instructor, I truly enjoyed Citizen Jane's attention, note taking, and insightful questions.

We had finished the section on trespass the week before and were traversing the mine field of Citizens Arrest. During the discussion phase Jane queried more in depth than in the past. I, as the instructor, was overjoyed because I had an actual live person who appeared to thirst for the good and solid core of basic information every free person should know, or at least I believe every free person should know.

This is information near the cornerstone of the freedom so many of us in Oregon hold almost in reverence. It was information I paid a dear price monetarily to learn and through the hard knocks of experience, which I considered for and in behalf of my clients and students. Sometimes I could not help but pause for just a moment to suck air in through the nose and out through the mouth, slowly, savoring the pinnacle of an instructor's joy; a student who actually gets it. And for the mere paltry sum of less than $40 for the term they could each drink of my wisdom!

That Thursday night as that class ended I gave everyone a "thank you" and gave each one of them two extra strong electrical ties. "Go forth and arrest but remember, as you use your rights you will face a small multitude of charges in tort such as false arrest, false imprisonment, and who knows what else." The electrical ties were thick, about a half an inch wide plastic 36 inches in length.

This class was at a place and time where in the county of Pandora the Pandorians were undergoing substantial road construction and improvements. The county had huge amounts of federal funding for the various projects but the funding had matching money, time, and performance strings.

As a cost and time savings measure Pandora Public Works had decided to forgo the 8 mile trip around various pieces of private property using the old road into the rock quarry/gravel pit, a total of 16 miles savings per trip. The chosen alternative was to go directly through Jane Smith's property, less than a quarter of a mile one way and a much better road.

When Pandora Public Works approached Jane with their request to use the road across her property she told them an unqualified "No." Pandora Public Works told Jane they were going to exercise their power of Eminent Domain and use the road anyway. They promised to fix it back up when they were done. With that, they moved in the rock crushers, dump trucks, and various other equipment needed to run the quarry. From then until my class Jane had objected several times to various people in the county including the sheriff and the county commissioners. All complaints had apparently fallen on deaf ears.

If crossing her property without permission was not enough, due to the shape of the hills at the back of her property, the sound of the rock crusher and other equipment funneled down as if it were directed at her home and her personally. The noise of the grinding and crushing rock started as early as 4:30 a.m. some mornings and ran as late some nights as 9:00 p.m.

None of this was known to me. So with ignorance and joy in having an actual live person in my class that night I proceeded with the elements of a Citizen Arrest. I had already taught the elements of what constitutes a trespass and when trespass crosses over, changes from civil to become criminal in its nature.

Also unknown to me but as a result of the class on Trespass, Jane had already painted a sign on a 4' by 8' piece of plywood, posting it at the front gate of her place. It said, **"NO TRESPASSING. No entry except by invitation, warrant, or exigent circumstances. All government people get a warrant before coming on this property. Jane Smith, OWNER."** It was dated and had her phone number on it.

That next morning, a Friday, after the various people who worked at the quarry/gravel pit had entered, Jane again locked the back gate effectively locking them away from her property (the first time they simply cut the lock off). It was about 7:30 a.m

Her good friend, who was also a relative, showed up right on time. He cut a deep trench across the road on her side of the fence with his backhoe, near where the road exited onto the county gravel pit. He parked the backhoe in the road, next to the trench, taking the key to the machine with him and went home. After he drove out the front gate, Jane's best friend who was a well thought of former county commissioner showed up, again right on time. She had shut the front gate behind her which was at Jane's request but had not locked it.

"What is this about Jane?"

"Let's just visit, you watch." Jane gave a nervous laugh which was not reassuring to Friend.

A four-door Dodge sedan entered the property driving up the driveway. They did not shut the gate they had opened. While they were opening the gate Jane had picked up her new cell phone. She called the sheriff's office and asked to be connected to emergency dispatch. "I have criminal trespassers and can figure no real reason why they would be here except to harm me in some way!" Dispatch was concerned and responsive. Jane noted she had a sign that said "No Trespassers." 911 told her to stay on the phone, "no matter what happens!" As a side note, this was when cell phones were the size of bricks, weighed about the same, and almost looked like gray bricks.

The car stopped. It was right in front of the steps up to her front porch. Two men were in the car, one in a suit, the other in some common work clothes. The suit got out, shrugged his faded brown sports jacket around a little. After coming up the steps Mr. Suit knocked on the door.

Jane opened it so fast it startled the man. He tried to recover as he looked at her 6'1" slender frame with no humor or smile on her face. If anything it was the opposite. He said, "I am Mr. Suit from Public Works."

Her response caught him trying to say something more. She almost yelled. "Can't you read?"

"Uh," he stuttered the word, "yes, I can read."

With brisk and short, clipped words Jane asked, "Did you see the sign? No trespassing!"

Again, "Uh," but with a little more control. "Yes. I saw the sign."

He was visibly uncomfortable. She said, "Then you are trespassing. Get out of here. Now. Get off my property!"

He manned up a little, "I am authorized, I..."

With more of the short, clipped words. She again almost shouting said, "Do you have a warrant?"

"Ah, No."

"Are you chasing a felon or someone you saw committing a felony?" she asked aggressively.

"No."

"Then you are trespassing. Get off my property." She pointed with the phone.

"I don't have to. I am from Public Works. I am authorized."

She said almost sweetly, "Just a moment." She turned away, putting the cell phone in her left hand. It had been held the whole time so that everything he said would be captured on the tape she knew was recording the conversation. She reached behind the door, came out with a handgun, pointed it at him, and started screaming. "On the ground, on the ground! You are under arrest."

I have personally been there before. Regardless of the caliber it looks like about a .75 monster.

She reported back to me that in the past she had never seen such fear in the eyes of another or been so fearful herself. As he laid on the porch she ordered him to put his hands behind his back. He did so without any comment, quickly. He kept looking at the car with the man sitting there, pleading in his eyes. She used one of the two electrical ties I had given each of my class members just the day before.

The cinch was tight. After just a moments contemplation, Jane then hogtied his feet to his hands with the second electrical tie. She yelled over to the man in the car, "Do you want to get out and be arrested or just follow us to the police station." Even though it was somewhat timid, he shouted through the window that was down, "I will follow you."

Jane told dispatch she had arrested the trespasser for criminal trespass. She said that she felt compelled to use the gun in self-defense because the fat guy was so much bigger than her and that she feared anyone who would disobey the laws designed to protect people like her by trespass on her property must have intended to hurt her.

She said she was bringing him into the satellite sheriff's station in Another Somewhere. She and her friend went out to load the man into her little Japanese pickup. Jane and her friend tried to lift him up but were unable to do so. They decided to drag him to the pick-up, just a few short yards away. Down the steps. Thump. Thump. Thump. Thump.

When they got to the back of the pickup, just as on the porch, they couldn't lift him up, but they tried mightily and did get him most of the way up. Jane, a country girl, did what she learned working in the fields bucking hay. She kneed him in the gut, over and over. Each time they got just a little closer to getting him in the pickup bed. After about the sixth time they had him far enough up they could get him into the bed of the pickup using his arms and legs as levers.

Mr. Public Works at first didn't say anything but before they finished loading him, he was cussing and swearing at them and his partner in the car. The bound man generally threatened Jane and everyone she ever knew with every kind of lawsuit he could imagine.

Another Somewhere, Pandora was a small community of less than

2,000 people. Everyone knew everyone else or was related to them. When Jane arrived at the satellite office, there was quite a crowd to watch the scene. She told the sergeant who was obviously in charge, "There he is. I will fill out any paperwork that needs to be done."

The sergeant was leaning on the body of the 4X4 Explorer, one of the sheriff's trucks. He just waived his head in a negative, arms folded across his too large belly. He pointed to the building, "In there."

Jane was first surprised, then she became exasperated. "Doug, are you sure, in there?" The sergeant just nodded a little "yes" with a small grin on his face.

Turning to her friend, "Come on, help me unload him."

The baggage was starting to shout. "No. Don't let the bitch touch me." From there he got a lot worse.

Just as Jane and Friend couldn't lift him up, when they went to drag him out, they dropped him as he cleared the tailgate because they couldn't hold him. Then they dragged him all the way into the building because they couldn't carry him, about 80 feet. Later I asked her, "Why didn't you just undo his feet?"

"Don, I didn't think of it. I was so mad. So very mad, and scared. And he was calling me the vilest names. And I was scared. I was trying to do everything right because I knew he was going to sue me."

There is a lot more to this story but for the purpose of a citizen's arrest it has all of the elements. First as Paul Harvey would say, "... for the rest of the story." The county agreed to fix Jane's road, including filling in and compacting the trench. They agreed to use the other road. Start time for the equipment would be after 7:30 in the morning and to stop all but the hauling trucks at 5:30 in the evening.

Mr. Public Works made it clear to county supervision he was going to sue Jane. Pandora County made it clear they were going to prosecute him for criminal trespass and if there was anything in the car that could be used as a weapon, the charge would be a felony III instead of a misdemeanor. He decided to drop the case. The county did also. It ended with Jane and her property secure from trespassers.

The elements of a citizen arrest are: The private person has to have the crime committed in their presence and they have to see it. Once the arrest has been made the arrested person has to be delivered up to a judge or to a peace officer by the person making the arrest without delay.[61]

In making the arrest the private person can use such force as is justifiable under the statutes in Oregon. A simple restatement of the statute is, "A private person may arrest another person for any crime committed in the presence of the private person if the private person has probable cause to believe the arrested person committed the crime. A private person making such an arrest shall, without unnecessary delay, take the arrested person before a magistrate or deliver the arrested person to a peace officer. In order to make the arrest a private person may use justified physical force as follows:

> Private persons acting on their own account are justified in using physical force upon another person when and to the extent they reasonably believe it is necessary to make an arrest or to prevent the escape from custody of an arrested person whom the person has arrested as outlined above. If the private persons are acting under the circumstances outlined above they are justified in using deadly physical force only when they reasonably believe it is necessary for self-defense or to defend a third person from what they reasonably believe to be the use or imminent use of deadly physical force against them or a another person in their presence."[62]

Public Policy – Natural & Fundamental Rights

Notwithstanding the federal and Oregon State Constitutional provisions, and the natural right of man to protect himself and loved ones, in the statutory development of the common law Oregon has taken a divergent direction dangerous to our constitutional civil rights. Nonetheless these statutes are upheld as current statements of the laws applied in Oregon.

The Oregon Legislative Branch of our state government has chosen through these same statutes to outline what they think the public policy should be concerning our fundamental right to protect ourselves. Those statutes are for the most part set forth in our web site and at various places on the web. See www.oregonconcealedlaw.com, which when clicked on will lead you to the laws for the actual language in this short workbook about the real application of the law to our right to carry personal protection in the form of handguns.

Therein they offer an outline whereby each of us can get a license to carry a concealed handgun in Oregon with the exceptions of certain felons, recent crime commissioners, and crazies who have been adjudicated a risk to themselves, others, or society. In the alternative, that same group of statutes allows us to openly carry a firearm for our protection. This is at least in part consistent with the recent Supreme Court cases called *McDonald* and *Heller*.[63] Those cases most simply stated say we have the right to be able to personally protect ourselves and our loved ones under the Federal Constitution. And we have the right to use handguns in doing so. According to the high justices, that means we have the right to have handguns in a condition that allows us to do so. Again, see the Oregon Legislature's view of these rights through its statutes, ORS 166.250 and 166.260.

The Oregon Executive Branch has made no real statement in its Administrative Rules one way or another about how it views our right to protect ourselves, but have simply defaulted to the other two branches of government. With that said, implicit in enforcement actions that are certainly optional to the Executive Branch officers, they sometimes most aggressively enforce those laws we are now talking about. The implicit part that can be drawn from that enforcement is that they buy in to the concept that the government has the right to limit our right to protect ourselves, and the right to limit how we will protect ourselves.

The Judicial Branch has rejected the Legislative Branch's statutory statements of what the public policy is[64] but has generally supported the laws. In a close reading of that rejection we find they are really rejecting the whole concept that the statutory scheme in Oregon is a public policy statement.

Both the Oregon and Federal Supreme Courts have said over and over that which the government can create, it can take away. It follows, the public policy in the above matters is as fickled as the government today, and the special interest crowd it will be representing tomorrow.

There is nothing in this short conversation about the "public policy" that is or should be reassuring to those who love freedom, and the forces that brought this great nation into being. However, it is the thrust of this book that we follow the laws of today as they are applied today. Understanding the public policy or lack of public policy driving these laws can help us form our own thoughts on the "who" of those we consider for election, and how we will view individual cases from the jury box.

A Personal Note about Judges and a Courthouse

I have nothing but the highest and even bitter contempt for Oregon presiding judges who pass judicial administrative regulations that keep honest people from carrying handguns for their personal protection in the courthouse and the courtroom. They violate their oath of office and no amount of legal mental masturbation can justify that contemptible practice, which in my perspective is a complete prostitution of themselves and their personal integrity to the other branches of government in violation of my fundamental constitutional right to be able to have immediate protection for myself and third parties in my presence.

At the time of this incident outlined below most of my general practice of law was in Douglas County. They had implemented a policy for the protection of the judges and staff to have an electronic search unit put up at the entries to the courtroom section of the Courthouse. It was/is one of those metal detectors we often see today.

On a particular day, I needed access to the law library which was down the hall on the right, the courtrooms being on the left. As I entered the hallway I had to go through the metal detector. I reasoned it did not matter whether I had anything metal because I was not going to the courts.

Compounding the disgust I felt for this intrusion on my constitutionally guaranteed right both federal and State, there were not one or two, but three fat, old, retired county sheriff deputies running the machine. They were designated "bailiffs." To provide further insight, I knew that as "retired" they were already receiving more out of the public till than most people in Douglas County who performed actual work. That was without the double dipping allowed in the Public Employment Retirement System.

There they were, so fat they couldn't do their jobs as officers of the law and could not do their real jobs as bailiffs. I saw and still see those machines guarded by incompetent fat people as symptomatic of some of the flaws in the system. The fat old farts cannot do their jobs so the machine helps compensate for their inadequacies by lessening their real functional responsibilities and putting each of us individually more at risk.

Even if they could have otherwise done their jobs as bailiffs, far too often in the courtroom environment they would fall asleep. Upon this tapestry I paint the rest of the story.

So there I was, gun in boot, keys in pocket, change in pockets, pen knife I used as a letter opener, etc. I actually thought that in going to the law library, I would get through the entry devices for my research purposes. I wasn't going to a courtroom. After all, they had two more bailiff/guards than needed. I could be escorted to the library if necessary. That thought was further supported by the fact I saw Assistant DAs and the DA repeatedly be allowed to circumvent "the machine!"

But alas we did not get to the gun when searched to enter that hallway. Each time I tried to go through the detector it would go off, and I would remove one more article of something, and put it in the little tub on the conveyor. Before we got to the gun, and after they had almost reached the limit of their tolerance for my antics I gave up. I think they became so frustrated because they actually had to do something regardless of how minimal it was.

The next day the court was closed. I went through the detector with no problems or issues. No one was there. I used my pass card to get into the law library. In the library there were a lot of books that no one looks at. In response to my curiosity and combined frustration I left another gun I carried in my briefcase that day behind some shelving on the floor, behind the old books on the north side of the library.

Two days later I went back to the courthouse yet again. This time court was in session. This time I made sure that I had no metal on me except my pen, belt buckle, and the steel instep protectors on my Tony Loma cowboy boots. I went through the metal detector with a breeze. I noted it was a different three officers, but again three of them, with two being retired. None of the officers were quite as fat as the officers from the other day. I wondered how the system could possibly afford five out of the six who were in such poor physical condition that it was visibly obvious they could not do the job.

In the library I retrieved my gun. I went into one of the courtrooms and "observed" for almost an hour before I left, with the gun still in my brief case. So much for security. I am sure with the publishing of this book Douglas County and other multiple use courthouses will reexamine their practices. But what this is really about is the contemptible judge who stomps on your and my constitutional rights. In reflection I believe they should be made to *enforce* our constitutional rights or in the alternative be disbarred.

Marijuana

I excerpted these quotes below to help provide a conceptual basic understanding of what a "concealed handgun license" is in Oregon in addition to understanding the current status of the attack on those who use marijuana medically and legally in Oregon. These excerpts are taken from a case involving whether a person with a medical marijuana card can have a license to carry a concealed handgun in Oregon:

We first met Paul Sansone at one of our booths this last summer (2011). Paul was frustrated. At that time he had a medical marijuana card as authorized under the laws of Oregon. Paul told us he had applied for a concealed handgun license through the sheriff in Washington County. Sheriff Gordon sent him a letter rejecting his application.

Paul went on to say, "I am left defenseless. You know what is worse, now I feel like a target, like I got a big f#^$#%& target on my back and the police are holding the gun!" He asked, "What can we do when the sheriff won't follow the law?" The conversation took some twists and turns but ended with Paul telling me, "I would not carry under the influence. I am not that stupid."

He of course asked in the process of the conversation for legal advice and direction. I steered him away from that request knowing that with my Form A resignation from the Oregon State Bar Association all I could do was get myself in trouble and possibly him too. I wanted to suggest for him to go back to his attorney and get a court writ compelling the action of Sheriff Gordon.

His case had wound through the Oregon court system ending in the Supreme Court combined with the case of Cynthia Willis. The combining of cases that have similar facts and issues of law is not unusual.

Cynthia had applied for her expired concealed handgun license to be renewed. Oregon is what is called a "mandatory" state in that when a person's renewal application has complied with all of the "stuff" in the statute the sheriff has a mandatory duty to issue the license just as the sheriff had that duty in Paul's case. And just as in Paul's case Sheriff Michael Winters in Jackson County refused to issue Cynthia her concealed handgun license.

Sheriffs Gordon and Winters relied on federal law in their rejections of Paul and Cynthia's applications for their concealed handgun licenses with the Oregon Court of Appeal noting:

> "[I]t shall be unlawful for any person [...] who is an unlawful user of or addicted to any controlled substance (as defined in section 102 of the Controlled Substances Act (21 U.S.C. 802)) [...] to ship or transport in interstate or foreign commerce, *or possess in or affecting commerce,* any firearm or ammunition; or to receive any firearm or ammunition which has been shipped or transported in interstate or foreign commerce." 18 USC § 922(g) (emphasis added). According to the sheriff, issuing a concealed handgun license to a person who admittedly uses marijuana, a Schedule I controlled substance under federal law, 21 USC section 801, would frustrate the purpose of the federal Gun Control Act.[65]

The court goes on to talk for pages in legalize but ending in a ruling in favor of Paul and Cynthia. The sheriffs appealed to the Oregon Supreme Court, again refusing to do their mandated duty.

The sheriffs renewed their same arguments before the Oregon Supreme Court. That court, again in a long document full of legalize found in favor of Paul and Cynthia and affirming the order of the Court of Appeal which in its turn had affirmed the order of the Circuit Court from which the chain of appeals started.

So bringing this to its logical conclusion, the state through the sheriffs' departments are required to issue the concealed handgun licenses to Paul and Cynthia notwithstanding Paul and Cynthia holding legal Oregon medical marijuana cards. Alas, not the conclusion. The sheriffs have appealed the decision of the Oregon Supreme Court to the Federal Courts on the same questions they have now heard the answer to in the three differing levels of actions in Oregon. Paul and Cynthia continue to wait for the sheriffs to do their mandated duty and as Paul related to me a second time, "I am left without the ability to protect myself."

From the cases: "ORS 166.291 to 166.295, the statutes pertaining to concealed handgun licenses, do not affirmatively grant a licensee the right to carry a handgun. Rather, as ORS 166.250(1) (a) exemplifies, the legal effect of a concealed handgun license is to exempt the licensee from state laws that would otherwise prohibit concealment of that firearm. See, e.g., ORS 166.173(2)(c) (city or county ordinances to regulate, restrict, or prohibit the possession of loaded firearms in public places as defined in ORS 161.015 do not apply to "[a] person licensed to carry a concealed handgun"); ORS 166.260(1)(h) (ORS 166.250 does not apply to "[a] person who is licensed under ORS 166.291 and 166.292 to carry a concealed handgun"); ORS 166.370(3)(d) (prohibition on possession of firearm in public building in ORS 166.370(1) does not apply to "[a] person who is licensed under ORS 166.291 and 166.292 to carry a concealed handgun"); ORS 166.663(2)(g) (statutory prohibition on casting artificial light while in possession of certain weapons does not apply when "the person has been issued a license under ORS 166.291 and 166.292 to carry a concealed weapon"). Thus, a concealed handgun licensee — marijuana user or not — is not affirmatively authorized to carry a firearm by way of Oregon's concealed handgun licensing statutes; what the licensing statutes do is provide an exemption from state criminal liability for concealing a handgun that the licensee independently has a right to possess." *Willis v. Winters*, 235 Or. App 615 (2010) 234 P.3d 141; see chapter 13 below.

(We of course think this analysis is flawed in the clear Oregon constitutional light shown by Article 1, Section 27 recognizing the fundamental right of each of us to bear arms in our defense without limitations as to whether the arms are rifles or pistols, concealed or carried openly.)

What this analysis by the courts show is the willingness of the courts to avoid the real underlying issue of whether the state of Oregon really has the authority to regulate concealed licenses or make declarations a license is a "requirement" to engage in otherwise lawful conduct authorized by the Oregon Constitution and reserved to us individually as a fundamental right.

As it currently stands, this matter surrounding lawful marijuana use in Oregon will not be settled until a final determination is concluded in the federal court system which will be sometime after this book is in print.

Paramilitary Activity

In almost every live class we are asked one or more questions about paramilitary activity, what constitutes such activity, and whether paintball gatherings are in fact a form of paramilitary activity.

Paramilitary activity is when three or more persons band together with one or more of the persons exhibiting, displaying, or demonstrating to the others how to make a firearm, explosive, incendiary device, or other techniques capable of causing injury or death to others. The person engaged in the described education has to know the education will be used unlawfully in a civil disorder.

In review of the statute and understanding the education will be used unlawfully I am almost flabbergasted that such criminal activity is linked in some form to "civil disorder." I guess being a country boy causes a different look. A pig dressed in a cute pink skirt, with pierced ears and ear rings, lipstick, and a bra is still just a pig. The difference between us simple folk and the sophisticated politically correct is that we would call the pig a pig. But back to the paramilitary activities.

This type of activity is extended to those who gather for practicing or being educated in these same examples of civil disorder. It is a Class C Felony. ORS 166.660.

The question then transforms into whether paramilitary activity includes paintball contests and maneuvers. The general answer is that this is NOT considered paramilitary activity. However, while the line is clear it is easy to cross. If those engaged in paintball sports are doing so for training and/or practicing so that they can more effectively engage in a civil disorder by unlawful means, they then would wade in the gray area of the law and potentially be at risk of engaging paramilitary activity.

The advice given to groups otherwise engaged in the sport of paintball for lawful purposes is not to worry. Before writing this portion of this book *Oregon Concealed* I took the opportunity to search the Oregon Legal Database. I could find no cases that addressed either "paramilitary activity" or "ORS 166.660." I think my advice of 17 years ago is still sound today.

CHAPTER 14

Another Political Commentary

There is a hierarchy of Oregon Laws somewhat like an inverted pyramid. One would think that foundational stone is the Oregon Constitution. It is. From there, the building of the pyramid's second layer is the Statutory and Common Laws of Oregon. The third layer is the Administrative Laws and Rules created by Administrative Agencies in Oregon. The forth layer is the Rules and Regulations. And of course, just as the heading of this chapter would lead you to believe, the last layer is the policies. The layers of the pyramid are bound by the glue of the Oregon Legislature, the Executive Branch, and the Judicial Branch of our government.

The reality is different as can be seen in the inverted pyramid. There are those who believe the pyramid will topple due to the abuses in creation of Oregon law. In 1991 through 1993 I lobbied against the Administrative Law system. During that period of time the Oregon Legislature considered about 6,000 changes and new laws. It enacted about 600. During that same period of time Executive Branch administrative agencies passed about 60,000 changes and new laws without any legislative review.

As onerous as that may sound, it gets worse. In a series of cases in the recent past the Oregon Supreme Court has said that these administrative rules have the same force and effect as if passed by the legislature. Having digressed, we move back to the original discussion.

The Oregon Constitution is a document whereby we as Oregonians have bound ourselves to a social compact.[66] We have collectively said we are willing to be governed by elected people. We set up a process for governance. Acceptable law becomes a process we agree to recognize.

We made reservations within the allowance of governance to insure that our fundamental rights and basic freedom would not, and even could not, be trampled. We do not ask you as the reader of this book to believe or disbelieve these statements. We do ask you to weigh these matters and if you have questions, to please research them. We are confident that if you have not already come to a conclusion you can live with, in time you will. We caution you in arriving at a conclusion you can live with, that it may be one whereby you commit your posterity to suffer slavery or die with as well as yourselves; the same price for your belief system as many of our founding fathers paid.

Projecting this thought forward and overlaid on the theme of this book, some people mistakenly, for whatever reason they choose, never look at the very foundation from which springs the role of law concerning handguns as they are applied today. I take this opportunity for the briefest of superficial looks to point us in a direction of possible understanding.

It is not a mistake to first look at the Federal Constitution of the United States of America. The history of the development of the Magna Charta, the eventual Bill of Rights, and flowing through European immigration to the Americans are the original amendments to the adopted Constitution of the United States. Those amendments originally left out of the Constitution were added because the framers came to understand, under the turmoil of the period, that what they had come to believe were fundamental rights of free men and a free nation needed to be protected, especially from the secret combinations of governments.

Foundational to securing a new understanding of the forerunner to the social compacts of today and the various state constitutions was the sure knowledge that guns, rifles, cannon, and pistols (arms) were essential in protecting us as a people from King George III. To preserve the ability to protect us from the throws of government, there was a universal recognition of the necessity for us to be able to keep and bear arms. Of worthy note is that there were no and are no limitations on "arms" from a constitutional view. As frightening as it is, that which the government has as its arms, that too belongs to us if we so choose.

As an outflow of that thinking came the generally recognized principal in the various state constitutions (www.oregonconcealed.law) what was otherwise understood as a matter of daily fact in the late 1700s. It was and is a right to protect ourselves, our family, others, and our property. As a fundamental thought that not only includes against the ravages of unrestrained government, but also against our fellow beings.

The federal Second Amendment of course provides us with the right to keep and to bear arms. Most people never know or forget the purpose of that language was to make sure we as a people, whether on an individual basis or collectively would never have to again bend to the tyranny and slavery of a governing force without the ability to protect ourselves from that tyranny and slavery.

We leap forward to the Oregon Constitution where not one but rather two provisions work for us to allow us to have that same ability our forefathers bought with their blood, lives, and fortunes. In the endnotes are listed those provisions, Article 1, Section 27 and Article 3, Section 1.[67]

Article 1, Section 27 is the right to keep and bear arms for our personal defense. It doesn't get much simpler. Here in Oregon we do not need the Federal Supreme Court *McDonald*[68] or *Heller*[69] cases to establish that right because we have already accomplished that through our own social compact.

Before leaping forward to current times and events we continue this brief pause to look again at Article 1, Section 1 and ask ourselves if we actually did in fact bind government with this document, can it then break those bonds. Of course the answer is unequivocal. It can. What flows from those broken bonds, the promises we made to ourselves and extracted by oath from all who serve, is an outlaw government when it steps beyond the bounds of the social compact.

Upon this tapestry we weave in the lightest colors Article 3, Section 1 (see Endnote 2) of our Constitution. Therein governance is limited in its scope, each branch being bound from doing the job of the other two. Now we simply step back to again view the pyramid. We suggest we have moved from a constitutional republic to a social democracy. I again ask you if you have the time to read *The Law* by Frederic Bastiat (www.constitution.org/cmt/bastiat/the_law.html). It is a simple read with clear principals easy to understand.

To the astute reader I took the above out of order to stay within the simple framework of the Articles of the Constitution before writing a little about the common law and statutory law.

I provide no proofs, having done the research a long time ago and I don't want to go down that path again. You too can do that research if you have an interest. What you will find is that Oregon's Judiciary eventually ruled with respect to Administrative Law that each branch of government had the right to make rules within its own branch for the administration and governance of its own employees.

From there the courts made a huge unconstitutional ruling that if a statute implied something that was not fully written, administrative agencies could fill in the blanks. The next step in the course of time was administrative agencies of the state could follow the dictates of the legislative branch and write rules wholesale as long as those rules were within the "scope" of the statutes. It reasoned the people elected to the legislative branch of government were just elected people, overworked, overstressed, and after all, during such short sessions every other year they could not possible get everything done in detail within the system.

In this approach by those governing is the failed concept the governance system was set up so that it could and would be curbed in that process through a system of checks and balances. The architects of the Federal Constitution intended to slow down the juggernaut of governance in its imposition of laws that are a direct attack on our constitutional concepts of individuals being free.

In repeating the above: In a period of gross judicial legislative action the Court of Appeal and the Oregon Supreme Court made a series of findings and rulings that held the "rules" written by the administrative branches of Oregon government had, and have, the same force and impact as if they had been written by Oregon Legislature[70] provided they were within the scope of the statutes. What these courts have not addressed and do not address is Article 3, Section 1 requiring a separation of powers between the three branches, except to say, and I paraphrase: "The legislature has failed to act. If we do not carve out an administrative process, we will lose federal governmental funds."

These cases created a view of Oregon as a national leader in the field of administrative law. At least that is the view as seen through the eyes of a significant portion of Oregon legislators. The theories were adopted across the nation limited to a minority of states. In its simplest terms a fox in the form of Oregon's Executive Branch was given the power to screw the chickens or eat them without any meaningful review by the Judicial Branch's power due to the fact the Judicial Branch subordinated itself to Executive Branch. Of course this could not have happened if the Legislative branch in prostituting itself to the other two branches had refused the role of a political whore.

Often times this was accomplished by mere recital of the lead Oregon cases and what it is perceived they stand for. For Oregon this series of cases were the last real nail in the coffin leading to the burial of the Separation of the Powers doctrine (see Endnote 2) of our government.

Now the Executive Branch of government accomplishes the Legislative job by making laws wholesale. It does the work of the Judicial Branch of Oregon's government through its Administrative Law judges, each of whom wishes he or she were a *real* Constitutional Article 7, Section 1 judge. And of course after the Executive Branch has made the law they rule on, they enforce the law through the administrative law judge paid by them.[71] It follows the doctrine for Separation of Power is dead.

We next briefly attend the Common Law. The Common Law arises out of old England. It is a system of law where by precedents particular rules and applications of law were established. This provided stability and understanding through a common sense application of those laws to the everyday things that happened in the criminal and civil environment of those days. From "then" until now those laws have slowly been codified, what we call the "statutory law."

All of the actual application of the gun laws I have talked about in this work are statutory in nature and in the world of law a recent creation. Some of the gun laws are merely codified common law while others are made up out of the whole cloth weaved by the Oregon Legislature justifying their existence, making you and I respectively safe and accountable to the Administrative Laws discussed above and in terror to the criminal law for exercising our constitution rights under Article 1, Section 27.

Last, we address "policies" as a part of the Administrative Law in this particular. All of the administrative laws have a required procedure that is mandatory if it is to have an impact on citizenry of Oregon. Outside of that structure are the policies of the quasi-agencies, schools, community colleges, local boards, etc. Those policies over time are slowly being recognized as binding, and to which we collectively and individually can be held accountable in the same manner as we are now held in the administrative law arena. Thus, organizations that are not even administrative branches of Oregon governance are now making their own administrative rules. The next step for the courts in Oregon will be to recognize those second tier rules as laws having the same force and impacts as laws made by the Legislative Branch of government.

We do not apologize for the shortness nor the bluntness of this commentary in that this book is by its very nature one concerning the application of the current law today in Oregon as defined by all of the laws mentioned above. The readers in preparation of the final compilation of this book without exception noted their fascination with the concepts outlined above. They expressed a universal interest in knowing more whether as Democrats, Republicans, Independents or "Other," how this can be a reality. Consistent with our purpose this is NOT a writing intended to be a law review article for jurists so it falls short of "proofs." But none of the information is new and with your own research you can come to your own understandings. Whether differing or supportive, I encourage you to email me you opinions: don@ochlc.com.

To the end which this is written, we move from how the law got to where it is today to the actual requirements under the current governmental scheme. I close this section with a second recommended reading: *The Tyranny of Good Intentions* by Paul Craig Roberts and Lawrence M. Stratton.[72] Last, we note there are Political Science courses surrounding this short chapter and Jeffersonian principals of governance that take a semester, 3 hours a week for 13 weeks. We suggest the reader will get out of a study of these principals what the reader puts into it, and with the availability of those courses he or she can expand their understanding to whatever level they desire.

Under the concept of a hierarchy of laws there is:

- Oregon and Federal Constitutional principles outline fundamental rights reserved to the citizenry.
- The federal and state governments are divided into three branches, each constitutionally reserving its powers solely unto that branch. They are:
- Executive
- Judicial
- Legislative
- We have Common Law and Statutory Law, the first recognized by the people and the latter created by the legislative body.
- Made up of whole cloth not a part of the constitutional allowance is the merging of those three branches under the guise of Administrative Law.
- While Administrative Law is abhorrent to our constitution, our judiciary has prostituted itself to the other two branches and through judicial created legislation has adopted Administrative Law as a fourth branch of Oregon's governance.
- Article I, Section 1 is the social compact for Oregon.
- Article 1, Section 27 is our fundamental right to keep and bear arms for our personal protection.

CHAPTER 15

The Challenge of Vigilance
or The American Way

Most of us have read about the political "deals" made behind closed doors. It should be enough to say I have personally seen such deals made and even by circumstance been a part of that process. Ahh, the American Way.

We at Oregon Concealed Co. (www.oregonconcealed.com) believe in a constitutional republic valuing the enumerated rights of the individuals, the freedoms talked about in this book. Especially the fundamental freedom guaranteed by the Federal Constitution's Second Amendment and by the Oregon Constitution's Article I, Section 27 to be able to protect ourselves and those we love.

Even so, recognizing the practical world of politics today, the focus of this book has been on what you, the reader, need to know to stay out of trouble under the current laws, notwithstanding their probable constitutional infringement on my and your enumerated fundamental rights.

In the interim Oregon Legislature for 2012 we took a role in protection of those rights. A Senator Burdick introduced legislation that would have restricted law-abiding citizens who carry concealed handguns from school grounds and public buildings. Senate Bill 1550 would have made it a felony to carry on school grounds. Senate Bill 1551 would have made it so that law-abiding citizens who legally carry concealed handguns could not carry on school grounds or in public buildings.

When those initially failed having died in committee, they were reintroduced by Peter Courtney as Senate Bill 1594. It actually came to a vote but was defeated along party lines.

On our website are a series of some of the testimony given by those of us here at Oregon Concealed Co. (www.oregonconcealedlaw.com) which in the behind-the-scenes follow-up we have been told had a significant impact.

I was recently told by one of the behind-the-scenes power brokers that my letters were personally insulting to Burdick and Courtney. I was reminded Burdick and Courtney are in positions of power where they can use the system against us as a company and possibly individually. I was reminded they have ways to move behind the public scene, to achieve their goals. Having been a small part of that kind of thing some time ago, I fully understand the delivered message.

I suggested that I and a lot of their constituency were insulted by their attempts to circumvent the Oregon Constitution.

CHAPTER 16

A Road to Enlightenment

It may not be about handguns, but it is about shooting.

Bearded Pete Goodell was called Whisky Pete for a reason. He made his own moonshine using the formula from the early American period of the late 1700s. Whatever he distilled, and if it was organic he could distill it, Whisky Pete would add enough tobacco chew cut straight off the plug for good color. He would then add just a pinch of arsenic to give it a little bite. Last he would add some fruit juice "to give it a little sweetness" just before he poured it up, usually apple concentrate. Pete noticed me once with this added tidbit, "You can't be too careful. I would hate to see anyone really go blind." Then he winked at me behind the coke-bottle thick glasses that made his eyes look so beady and continued, "... but there is nothing like good apple juice!"

Of course my thoughts turned immediately to the arsenic. But he clarified for me on this occasion, "Too much of this peach juice (juice from the home-canned peaches his wife Ethel made) can wreck the whole thing."

Whisky Pete gave me my first muzzle-loading rifle in 1972, a .45 caliber Numrich Arms Hopkins & Allen Heritage model underhammer. With it he asked me, "When you are ready to graduate, will you make sure you give this here gun to someone else who is interested in black powder shooting?" I was humbled. We went outside off his back porch where he taught me to shoot it.

"I always blow down the barrel the first time just to make sure it doesn't have a blockage. That thing down there is called a 'nipple' and when ya blow through it, air is supposed to come out." Pete added power from a horn he had. He put a patch over the end of the barrel and rammed a .45 caliber round ball down the barrel with the appropriately named "ramrod." Lifting the gun he turned it upside down and handed it to me. "Here." Pete handed me a cap. "Put this here cap on that nipple." Pointing.

It was obvious how it was to fit, and being experienced in reloading for cartridge rifles, I did just that. "Now just cock the hammer back, aim it, and shoot the damn thing." Pete pointed at a flat rock about 3 inches across. It was on the side bank of a road cut about 30 yards away.

I rolled the gun back upright so the sights were on top. I wondered if it would shoot as I took aim. KaBOOM! The rock broke into four or five pieces. And I was hooked. There are too many stories to tell, maybe someday another book.

For Christmas I talked my wife into making a purchase for me. She bought a Civil War replica .58 caliber Mississippi rifle brand new for $67 as advertized in *Shotgun News*, a gun enthusiast publication. The box under the Christmas tree was a little box. It had a picture of the gun yet to arrive. Later in the spring of 1973 I gave the Hopkins & Allen underhammer to another who was just starting into black powder shooting.

That fall I shot the 5-shot 50-yard off-hand rifle match at the Jed Smith Rendezvous using that musket (at Josephine County Sportsman's Park). After four shots, I had a 40-4X. Exactness in repetition is the key to success. I lined up for the fifth shot, ending with a 48-4x. Steve Vincent or Spook as he was known in the black power circles, took first with a 50-5X. Andy Fathering took second with a 50-2X. Cabot Clark took third with a 49-3X. I took fourth.

While I am not always known to have the sharpest skinning knife, some things had become transparent over time. The best of shooters cannot shoot any better than their equipment allows without some luck. So I made the commitment to upgrade my competition rifle. Luckily for me, my musket rifle barrel would fit an original Whitney of the Civil War period.

Joe Williams of Springfield, Oregon (now Oregon Gun Works) wanted my barrel so he could put it on his original Whitney with the thought being he could take it to musket matches and shoot competitively. Later with the original barrel he could restore the Whitney back to its original condition and its value as an antique. I traded my barrel to Joe for another barrel as a replacement for me and $100. I sold my Mississippi for another $100 and used the $200 to buy parts for a new Hawkins-style mountain rifle I made over the 73–74 winter. It had a Cherry Corner's Lock, Long double set trigger, and a 34" 1 in 66" twist Douglas premium 3X barrel, all of the functioning parts to produce the core of quality.

All of that is to say I bought quality parts so I could have a quality gun if I assembled it correctly. I did and it was.

The Hawkins-style rifle was ready to go except for sighting it in when No Power, York, Spotted Bear (Jack Cook now of back east, John Toomer of Alaska, and Arnold Queener of Cottage Grove, Oregon) and I went to the Tioga Mountain Men's first annual shoot. I had an opportunity to shoot a couple of "sighting-in" shots before we started the trail walk.

A trail walk is a course of walking travel in which we stop at various stations to shoot for score. The targets are most often "primitive" which means we shoot as such things as metal devices called gongs. They make a ringing sound when they are hit. Other targets include such things as a string or feather to shoot in to two pieces, tacks to drive into a tree, or board with the ball shot from the gun; tooth picks with marshmallows where the goal is to shoot the marshmallow off from the tooth pick without breaking the toothpick. These are just a few of the targets. There are a huge number of different kinds of primitive targets.

The Tioga Mountain Men's course was challenging and fun. In part it was fun because with a little "Kentucky windage" I hit almost all of the targets, taking first overall. Our gang did well taking three of the first five positions. Of course there was the usual grumblings as there is with any club when another club shows up and takes most of the good prizes. To their credit at the fall shoot of the Fort Umpqua Muzzleloaders the Tioga Mountain Men showed up and did the same thing to us.

From there I worked with my muzzleloader and pistol every day. I studied and learned. I watched the best of the best in the Pacific Northwest, observing what they did differently than what I was doing, sometimes asking for pointers on one thing or another. Sometimes my wife would complain that I loved my gun more than her because the last thing I would do before nightly prayers, before going to bed at night was to engage in off-hand sighting practice at a target I had on the wall. This practice usually took about 20 minutes. Holding and sighting practice was also the first thing I would do in the morning before starting my day.

For actual practice, hunting, and competition with the muzzleloader I shot 82.5 grains of G&O FFF black powder. There are 7,000 grains to the pound which meant that for every pound I was shooting approximately 85 shots. By the end of 1974 I was shooting about 4 kegs of powder —100 pounds—or 8,500 shots a year.

In 1976 I went to the McKenzie Raiders spring shoot. The first prize was a $500 sponsorship to the national championships in Friendship, Indiana. Spook and the Deacon each shot a 50–5X in the 50 yard off-hand target. My group was a little tighter than his so I was awarded first in that shoot. Yes, my mountain-man name is "the Deacon." I took three firsts and three seconds in the aggregate. Spook took three firsts, two seconds, and one third. For business reasons neither of us could go to Friendship for the national championships. That day, the person who took third made the trip to Indiana. There he took the Mountain Man of the year award and overall championship.

In late November of 1976 the Fort Umpqua Muzzleloaders—through me—sponsored their then annual Turkey shoot. Having sponsored the 1975 live turkey shoot, we had vowed never to do that again. The blood and guts of that shoot is again, for another book at a later date.

One of the targets on this blustery cold and sometimes rainy day was a 2X4 contraption with crossed strings set at 40 yards. One string was on the back side of the 2X4s. The other was on the front. The object was to shoot the 2 strings, cutting both of them with 1 shot. As the sponsor of this target and as range master I was not shooting. The entry fee for this target was $1 with a re-entry fee of $.50 if the 8 available Butterball turkeys were not taken in the first round. The round was of course started with a draw for shooter numbers so that no one could complain about favoritism in the event all of the turkeys were won before the end of the first round. There were 24 shooters.

To make the target a little more difficult the strings were not tight. My thought was that with the air shock wave that precedes a round ball, if the shot were not perfect the string would roll around the ball, which in the test of the actual shooting is exactly what happened.

By the time everyone had shot the third round, there was such a bemoaning of the difficulty of the target; "No one can get this." "It's impossible." "We are throwing our money away." York, one of my best friends, actually was in my face at one point telling me how unfair the target was, and saying it couldn't be done. You have guessed it, not one turkey had been won.

York and I had been known to stand side by side in adversity. On one occasion when someone had called him a "nigger," he physically restrained me from the attack I was going to put on that person. As an aside from the story, John had taken the name York as a namesake after the first black man to come West who was with the Lewis and Clark expedition.

Knowing us for being "brothers" the men around the fire enjoyed the show with York whining and complaining. I was surprised at the verbal attack by York but in looking back he had talked about how he was going to win all of the turkeys so he was probably feeling a little put upon himself.

I commented. "John, you have all had three shots. I am willing to bet with you. Give me three shots and with one of them I will cut both strings." I was looking at him, eye to eye, man to man.

"How much?"

"Anything you want John." I was feeling peaceful, comfortable, at one with the situation. I didn't feel smug but something in me triggered him. John was known to rarely bet unless he had stacked the deck in his favor. His knee-jerk response was, "Two dollars! You get three shots to cut both strings with any one of those shots, just like the rest of us. Then I get my two dollars." And with that he backed off laughing.

York too had made his own muzzleloader from parts. Some of the shooters had named their guns. York simply called his "girl." When asked why, he would respond something like, "She makes me feel soooo good when I fondle her." I had not named mine. It was a rifle, an extremely accurate gun and as a tool could work wonders in the right hands.

I went over to the rack, picked up the shooting pouch, and the "gun." Most of the men now standing around with interest were true primitive shooters. I remember turning toward the shooting line and catching Stumpy's eye (Al Stromme from out Eugene way). He wore his custom-made, rawhide wide-brimmed hat that in the drizzle of the day had started to droop a little. Al's nod of encouragement was almost imperceptible.

The next set of eyes to engage me was Iron Rod (Jack Flint). He was a nemesis of sorts, having a different philosophy toward black powder events than most of us who were hard core primitive. Little did I know he would soon be replacing me as the club president. I was surprised with his grin of anticipation and nod in support too.

Focused on the two slightly drooping strings without thought I went through the mechanics of loading the gun, something I had by then done thousands of times before. I took a stance, closed my eyes, brought the gun up, and embraced my shooter's pose. I opened my eyes to find that I was aimed slightly to the right of where the strings crossed. Again without thought I moved my back foot to the right just a little while putting the gun down. Relax. Relax. It was not a thought, just a habit. Sucking air slowly in through nose, out through the mouth.

I again raised the gun and before bringing it to bear on the target closed my eyes, again. When I opened them, my sight pattern was possibly half an inch to the left of where I wanted it. I adjusted the heel of my left foot ever so slightly. The pattern aligned.

Not trusting it, understanding I may have made the adjustment with my arms, I put the gun down for the third time. I could hear York talking but could not understand what he was saying as I narrowed the focus on two crossing strings. When I brought the gun up for the fourth time and reopened my eyes, the sight pattern was right. I put the gun down, resting the steel butt on my moccasined right foot. Using the ramrod I outlined the toe of each foot in the moist red, clayed dirt.

Breathing is an art in competitive shooting. Deeply in through the nose, out through the mouth with, as those who practice Zen would say, "an empty mind." The heart slows. With longer between heartbeats, the shooting pattern can be held longer without the heart's pump surge throughout the body.

As I took a deep breath I raised the rifle while cocking it. Shouldering the Hawkin I pulled the back trigger setting it, and breathing slowly out it came to bear on the target perfectly during that sweet null spot where the heart is waiting to beat again. I would have almost two seconds before it beat again. The truly hair trigger was unconsciously touched. With the KaBoom I knew I had missed even though I could not see the target because of the billowing, burnt-gray smoke coming out of the barrel. The slight breeze took the smoke away but before there was again clarity I could now hear York. "I knew you couldn't do it!" I looked over at him. He was actually dancing a little jig. I couldn't help it. I smiled. Looking back at the target, one string had been cut in two. The other was frayed.

After racking the rifle I closed the range and we went out to the target. I reset it by cutting off the old strings and putting new ones on just like before. Everybody returned to the firing line. I reopened the range, recovered my rifle, turned it up so the barrel was pointing down.

I wanted to make sure there was no corn meal in it. None came out. I didn't put it past York to have plugged the gun so it wouldn't shoot the next shot. We had done that to No Powder once at a McKinzie Raiders' shoot. It was funny, then. Later York admitted to me he hadn't thought of doing that to me or he would have tried.

I toed the outline with the now loaded the rifle, and went through the competitive motions again. This time as I came down on the new target, I became one with it. When the gun went off, almost to my surprise, I knew I had busted both strings. From the KaBoom to the obscurity of the black powder smoke was an eternity. During that short period before seeing the actual result many things became known to me as a matter of personal knowledge instead of belief.

The eternity of that moment still impacts my life today. As I sit here writing I cannot help but relive that moment. In some ways I am sorrowful it was wasted on someone so young. I was only 29. It was not until I was late in my 40s I came to understand those enlightened understandings could be grown.

Rather than attempt to share the gleanings and understandings so personal to me, I close with this: Practice, Practice, Practice. Practice with your handgun. That can mean the difference between life and death for you or a family member. The act of target shooting can provide you with hours upon hours of family time, a bonding. And, regardless of religion or lack thereof, it can bring you to understandings of self, those around you, and your roll in the broader scheme of things.

I believe in the fundamental nature of man to be free from those who would impose their unrighteous will upon him or her. To that end, and in hopes this is not too offensive, as a Constitutional Patriot with a Mormon heritage and Zen understandings I pray for your ability to secure unto yourself and those you love the ability to be free and to stay free.

Note: A state constitution study

As an attorney who no longer practices law I have come to the conclusion the law is intended for all of us; not just those who have attended law school, not just those who have politically bought their way into the judiciary, not those who have reserved unto themselves the right to interpret the law (attorneys who become judges). The law is intended for all of us, with its natural meanings and understandings.

Part of what brought me to this conclusion was standing before a female judge. The judge could have been male. I have been in front of male judges every bit as incompetent, perhaps even more so. The only difference between them and this particular judge is the fact she wore her emotions on the sleeve of her tunic, that, and she lacked any measurable judicial integrity.

I wondered how she became a judge. Later through quiet investigation I found she was appointed to fill a vacancy. After careful review of the facts, talking to some politically astute Democrats (she was a Democrat) I found the predecessor male judge who "retired" did so timely so this particular female could be appointed to fill his vacancy. The political thought was that with his timely retirement it was time to appoint someone who could then run for the "elected" office of judge as an incumbent. The party wanted a woman with some years of experience because it was the political time for such appointments. Being somewhat experienced at life and having generally measured the level of her ineptitude I had the thought, *I wonder how many she had to sleep with to get that appointment.*

But regardless of the underlying "why," the appointment was granted. Note this is not a condemnation of Democrats. This judge and the political process could have just as easily been a Republican whore (within this meaning, the word "whore" is non-gender specific relating to the acts as opposed to the gender or sexual orientation of the appointee).

Remembering I practiced throughout the state of Oregon I found a number of judges who generally fit one of the roles commonly identified in another profession. *Those who can, do. Those who cannot, teach.* In the world of attorneys, those who can, do. Those who cannot, become judges.

There are differing thoughts on how the construction of various states' constitutions are to be applied to the concepts that we each have the inherent ability to keep and bear arms to protect ourselves, our families, and others against the unlawful acts of those who would deprive us of these protections. The criminal element, whether they be those who would enslave us through theft of our lives, portions of our lives, or political enslavement are the intended target of these constitutional provisions, and rightly so.

I have toyed with the idea there is a theme within the constitutions of the United States, under the Federal Constitution. To an understanding there might be such, I did a down and dirty internet research of the various constitutions of the states. The quick research shows us there is a commonality amongst most of the states in how our social compacts (state constitutions) are viewed as well as under the Federal Constitution.

It varies from a position of no individual constitutional state protections for the right to keep and bear arms, such as in a state like Minnesota, to a state like Nebraska where the constitutional provision not only provides for the right to keep and bear arms but within the provision provides for our use of arms in defense in a broad range of circumstances such as for defense of self, family, home and an undefined "others," including but not limited to security, recreational use, hunting, and all other lawful purposes.

Somewhere in between are states such as Massachusetts where their constitution speaks to people being born free with unalienable rights. It goes on to say that within those rights is the ability to defend their lives and liberties, and for seeking and obtaining safety and happiness.

Their constitution does not talk about how its citizenry or people are supposed to be able to defend themselves. Given the very fundamental foundation upon which this nation grew and the role Massachusetts played, which history was ripe with people who in their time were considered terrorists by the King of England; and by the use of arms including all of which were available to the citizenry at that time. With force of might these terrorists challenged the very fabric upon which governments of those days were founded.

Upon this rock some states such as Idaho, Iowa, and others take yet another view. They incorporate into their constitutions individual protections to protect ourselves and embrace the Federal Constitution (read that as Second Amendment) as the supreme law of the land.

Even within these constitutions there are several that allow the state to create restrictions on carrying concealed. The constitutional provision of Colorado, Idaho, Kentucky, and others reserve this power to control the circumstances of lawful "concealed carry" within their state by legislative mandate.

What I believe but as of yet has not been discussed on the internet, or at least that I have not yet found, are the enabling agreements between the various states with the federal government. I cannot believe the federal government would allow any state to join the union of states where the feds would give up supremacy and eminent domain issues. I believe within the various agreements we call "social compacts," and sometimes take for granted, are the core principals holding the federal constitution supreme. I am led to the hypothesis at a minimum this probably means the Second Amendment is alive and well in all of the states of the "union of states," or the United States of America as it is now called.

In making the circle to close this discussion; history tells us what the Second Amendment is all about. Any judge, whether a United States of America Supreme Court Judge or a local district court judge that rules against our individual fundamental right to keep and bear arms, or to limit our ability to keep and bear arms, commits acts of treason as defined in both the Federal Constitution and for us here in Oregon the Oregon Constitution.

In providing the brief research for your thoughtful pondering; and for the motivated, a starting place for research: If you find anything you think might be of interest in this matter or other areas of the treatment of our individual rights, I invite you to email me at don@ochlc.com.

CHAPTER 17

Wisdom in Summary
– The Pearls

Deadly Force

- Most people are mentally NOT prepared to defend themselves or others; and thus,
- <u>After</u> the confrontation of unlawful felony force being used against them have to take the time to make the decision; and
- Then after the decision has been made, have to start the physical process of defense; and
- Only after the first two steps do they become prepared in actuality to defend themselves or others.
- Justified force that is "deadly force" by a person in response to unlawful force is authorized when the intent or likely outcome of the confrontation is death or serious bodily harm but the person using a justified response may only use the degree of force which the person believes is reasonable under the circumstances.
- A justified defensive force is only allowed for the period of

time the Bad Guy is wrongfully using force that is intended or likely to cause death or serious injury to another in the presence of the person using defensive force.

- To use defensive deadly force which is sometimes otherwise called "self-defense"; the defensive person must reasonably believe their response is justified because the attacker engaged in an unlawful use of physical force.
- Sometimes the choice of whether to use self-defense can be whether to be tried by 12 or carried by 6.
- Be the first to call 911;
- Don't show the gun unless you intend to use it;
- Comply with the instructions of the officers;
  - Use the magic language, *I feared for my life*;
  - Use the magic language, *I want an attorney*;
- Admit nothing unless compelled;
- Deny everything if compelled;
- Counter charge (if it can be done without admitting anything).
- The situation of mutual combat modifies when one can and cannot use a gun in self-defense or defense of another. Do not engage in mutual combat.

Deadly Force Limitations

161.219 Limitations on use of deadly physical force in defense of a person. Notwithstanding the provisions of ORS 161.209, a person is not justified in using deadly physical force upon another person unless the person reasonably believes that the other person is:

(1) Committing or attempting to commit a felony involving the use or threatened imminent use of physical force against a person; or

(2) Committing or attempting to commit a burglary in a dwelling; or

(3) Using or about to use unlawful deadly physical force against a person. [1971 c.743 §23]

161.225 Use of physical force in defense of premises. (1) A person in lawful possession or control of premises is justified in using physical force upon another person when and to the extent that the person reasonably believes it necessary to prevent or terminate what the person reasonably believes to be the commission or attempted commission of a criminal trespass by the other person in or upon the premises.

(2) A person may use deadly physical force under the circumstances set forth in subsection (1) of this section only:

(a) In defense of a person as provided in ORS 161.219; or

(b) When the person reasonably believes it necessary to prevent the commission of arson or a felony by force and violence by the trespasser.

(3) As used in subsection (1) and subsection (2)(a) of this section, "premises" includes any building as defined in ORS 164.205 and any real property. As used in subsection (2) (b) of this section, "premises" includes any building. [1971 c.743 §25]

161.229 Use of physical force in defense of property. A person is justified in using physical force, other than deadly physical force, upon another person when and to the extent that the person reasonably believes it to be necessary to prevent or terminate the commission or attempted commission by the other person of theft or criminal mischief of property. [1971 c.743 §26]

161.270 Duress. (1) The commission of acts which would otherwise constitute an offense, other than murder, is not criminal if the actor engaged in the proscribed conduct because the actor was coerced to do so by the use or threatened use of unlawful physical force upon the actor or a third person, which force or threatened force was of such nature or degree to overcome earnest resistance. (2) Duress is not a defense for one who intentionally or recklessly places oneself in a situation in which it is probable that one will be subjected to duress. (3) It is not a defense that a spouse acted on the command of the other spouse, unless the spouse acted under such coercion as would establish a defense under subsection (1) of this section. [1971 c.743 §34; 1987 c.158 §22]

- Sometimes the sound of the gun is enough.
- In situations where a person has engaged in a mutual combat, a person is NOT justified in the use of force rising to a level of deadly force as a means to end the conflict.

Travel

- If one has a concealed handgun license they can carry concealed while traveling the highways and byways of Oregon and they can carry the concealed handgun loaded. They can also carry the handgun in the glove box or console.
- This includes not only the highways and byways of Oregon, but parking lots, and driveways generally open to the public.
- If a person expects to keep his or her driveway private, it must be properly posted or secured so as to give notice of the intent to keep it private.

The Stop

- It is recommended both by the NRA and by Oregon Concealed Co. that for the purposes of a stop the driver puts his hands at the 11:00 position on the steering wheel and carefully follows the instructions of the officer.
- The "stop" starts when the blue and red lights come on.
- The "trial" starts when the blue and red lights come on.
- The enforcement officer looks for admissions.
- If you feel compelled to speak,
  - Admit nothing.

- Deny everything.
- Counter charge.
- If the licensed person in the vehicle is carrying a concealed handgun, it should not be accessible to an unlicensed person in the vehicle.
- The trial starts when the lights go on.
- The COP is NOT your friend.
- The DA is not your friend.

Concealed

- The prohibition in ORS 166.250 is against carrying a concealed firearm. Enforcement officers generally consider a handgun concealed if it is out of their view.
- For a handgun to be concealed enforcement has to be able to prove through evidence that the person charged with unlawfully carrying a concealed firearm had an "intent" to conceal the handgun.
- "Concealed" has its common meaning as found in dictionaries: Generally that means the handgun was hidden or secreted from view with the unlawful intention for it not be seen or found.
- It is our recommendation the licensed person carrying a concealed handgun keeps it concealed, which includes not sharing information about having a handgun or where it is located with passengers.
- Oregon has an "accessible" statute which carries the presumption a handgun in a vehicle is available to those in the vehicle.
- We recommend the licensed person keep the handgun on their person,
    - or in a place where the passengers cannot get to it,
    - and the passengers are not told about it.
- Another exception to when a handgun is concealed is when one is carrying to and from a gun range:
    - The range needs to be one designed or used for handguns.
    - A person has to have a membership in the range.
- The person must be traveling to and/or from the pistol range.

- It is generally unlawful to carry a handgun loaded and/or concealed on the highways and byways of Oregon.
- Firearms carried openly in belt holsters are not concealed within the meaning of ORS 166.250(3).

Pearls

- From Contemporary Stories above you have learned that in Oregon all handgun discharges are initially treated as if they are the result of criminal activity.
- Shootings resulting in death are initially treated as homicides.
- Do not ask others if they are carrying a concealed handgun; do not tell others you are carrying a concealed handgun; and do not show the concealed handgun to others.
- Application of the mantra "Practice, Practice, and Practice" is your friend.
- Read, study, and learn about all aspects of carrying a licensed concealed handgun.
- "Reasonable belief" will usually be tested by a judge, jury, and/or a District Attorney.
- Sometimes the reasonable belief has to be or become the defensive shooter's reality in only fractions of a second.
  - "I feared for my life" is worth knowing and using; or
  - "I was in fear for third party's life."
  - "I want an attorney before any further questioning" is also worth knowing and using.
- "Son, no amount of education can compensate for a lack of common sense."
- If you lack common sense, you should not carry a gun.
- Enforcement thinks in terms of *you used a gun so you are a bad guy*!
- Your attorney is not your friend (but sometimes the best you can do under the circumstances).
- A competent attorney licensed to practice law in Oregon is one who when he or she gives you bad advice, you can sue them and have a resource called the Oregon State Profes-

sional Liability Fund where you can collect the remedies awarded you for the bad advice.

The Handgun

- In Oregon a handgun is generally loaded when it has any cartridges in it.
- There are exceptions in Oregon for persons carrying on an ATV.
- Persons with a concealed licensed can carry both concealed and loaded whether on their person, in or on an ATV.
- On an ATV if the person does NOT have a concealed handgun license, the handgun must be secured and locked in such a way as the person does not have direct access to the handgun. If it is secured in this manner, then:
  - Handguns are not loaded when the firearm is a revolver, when there is no live cartridge in the chamber that is aligned with the hammer of the revolver; or
  - When the firearm is a muzzle-loading firearm, when the firearm is not capped or primed; or
  - If the firearm is other than a revolver or a muzzle-loading firearm, when there is no live cartridge in the chamber.

Citizen's Arrest

- The elements of a citizen arrest are: The private person has to have the crime committed in their presence. Once the arrest has been made the arrested person has to be delivered up to a judge or to a peace officer by the person making the arrest without delay.
- In making the arrest the private person can use such force as is justifiable under the statutes in Oregon. A simple restatement of the statute is, "A private person may arrest another person for any crime committed in the presence of the private person if the private person has probable cause to believe the arrested person committed the crime. A private

person making such an arrest shall, without unnecessary delay, take the arrested person before a magistrate or deliver the arrested person to a peace officer. In order to make the arrest a private person may use justified physical force as follows:

- A private person acting on their own account is justified in using physical force upon another person when and to the extent they reasonably believe it necessary to make an arrest or to prevent the escape from custody of an arrested person whom the person has arrested as outline above. If the private person is acting under the circumstances outlined above they are justified in using deadly physical force only when they reasonably believe it necessary for self-defense or to defend a third person from what they reasonably believe to be the use or imminent use of deadly physical force against them or another person in their presence."

A Little about the Law – The System

- Oregon and Federal Constitutional principles outline fundamental rights reserved to the citizenry.
- The federal and state governments are divided into three branches, each constitutionally reserving its powers solely unto that branch. They are:
  - Executive
  - Judicial
  - Legislative
- Made up of whole cloth not a part of the constitutional allowance is the merging of those three branches under the guise of Administrative Law.
- We have Common Law and Statutory Law, the first recognized by the people and the latter created by the legislative body.
- While Administrative Law as it is applied in Oregon is abhorrent to our constitution, our judiciary has prostituted itself to the other two branches and through what is called

judicial legislation created law as a fourth branch of Oregon's governance.

- Article I, Section 1 is the social compact for Oregon.
- Article 1, Section 27 is our fundamental right to keep and bear arms for our personal protection.

This and Other Writings

As the author of this book, *Oregon Concealed*, I came to this endeavor by recognizing a "need" through people I represented. For the most part they were and are good people who received bad information. The brother-in-law, a former police officer, the neighbor, all of whom were also good people with good intentions knew "something" about handgun laws. Unfortunately their information was NOT clear and it was not an accurate statement of laws and rules designed to protect all. Generally other works we often rely on are loaded with legalese. They are difficult to read and even more difficult to understand; even with a legal background!

These matters you have taken the time to read and understand are important. Sometimes solid accurate information will be a foundational piece to help you and your friends (you will now be able to give "good" backyard advice) keep out of jail or even out of prison.

At this time I am contemplating a second book of examples. This will NOT be a compilation of incidents through my practice of law. I am interested in your story. I am looking for factual stories from contributing authors who can show the positive impact (no pun intended) supporting wise use of a handgun or lessons learned from basic breaches of protocols. You can email me at don@gmail.com, find me on Facebook, and on Twitter. I can also be found blogging around. For those who want a direct conversation, I can be reached at 541-579-3500 Pacific Coast Time Zone between the hours of 5:00 p.m. through 7:00 p.m. weekdays or emailed, "A comment or story" to Don (don@ochlc.com).

Over the years I have written mostly for personal enjoyment. Recently the decision to publish via the internet was made. In about 3 months a science fiction fantasy will be published about a witch searching for revenge to fill the feelings she has for the loss of her daughter. She knows in her heart revenge can lead to a dark place. Dawn refuses to look into that dark place until forced. There she finds an evil she cannot embrace. As she works her way back to sanity, she again embraces revenge, trying to anchor her soul to a reality she can live with as the forces of good and evil continue their ever conflicting need for balance. Look for *When Dragons Weep*. If you have an interest, drop me a note.

This fall the first of a 4 part book series will be released. Each book is a complete story. This meets one of my personal needs in that I do not like books with lingering endings. In this series each book is a contemporary story about a man who desires normalcy. "Larry" as a directed governmental sociopath agent is of course conflicted but not in any traditional way. He is modeled after a relative who has been clinically defined as having no conscience. Watch for *Remorse, No Remorse, Retribution*, and *Redemption*. *Redemption* is the last of the 4 books and soon to be finished 1st draft). With a little luck each will follow the other in about 4 to 5 month periods starting in about November of this year, 2012.

After this series of books, a hard core science fiction I completed a few years ago will be released, *Joseph Bringer*. After release from the wars as an injured veteran Bringer finds a new path for his broken body as "Arcodian," becoming a philosopher and wanderer. Like many from my generation (Vietnam) and the modern warriors of today, our views have been colored by the events of our past. Bringer in his new persona as Arcodian comes to recognize some truths about the fundamental nature of Man. He is confronted with the ancient but real world natural law that a prophet in his own land is without honor.

I am looking forward to my projects. I give thanks to each of you who have supported me by obtaining a copy of *Oregon Concealed*, and your commitment to a better society. Remember the box holding and maintaining freedom is first the voter's box, then the jury box. If they fail, there is the cartridge box. May your God go with you.

—Don
84058 N. Pacific Highway
Creswell, Oregon 97424
don@ochlc.com
541-579-3500

Support

Once the decision has been made to write a book, perhaps the easiest part of the process leading to publishing is writing the book. I started sometime in November of 2011. I finished the first rough draft in March of 2012. At approximately 66,000 words that is less than 1,000 words a day or less than 2 typewritten pages per day. The choice was made to limit the insertion of actual law in the book. Between the law and other supporting material there are approximately 120,000 additional words on our website at www.oregonconcealed.com. My personal experience has taught me that unless one is an attorney they usually are not interested in all of the legal support "stuff." It is there on our website for those who do want to read and know it.

What the readers taught me was most people do not want their reading experience interrupted by support material. They really did not want footnotes seeing those as an interruption in the page. For the visionary final approach I went to endnotes. The demographic of our student population has shown us most are more mature. For that reason the actual printed book is in a larger type.

In this process I have had several readers and initial proof readers. When I was searching for answers to questions about publishing, the Internet was probably the most useful tool in the process. Through networking and mentor/writer Linda Clair of Eugene, Oregon: I found Smashwords. Through Smashwords I found several people who were willing to digitize the book to meet Internet publishing standards. Of those offered by Smashwords for consideration I chose Maureen Cutajar at gopublished.com. I feel lucky in the choice process and I am well pleased with this selection and what she has accomplished for me.

I appreciate all of those who through their support have made this endeavor possible. To each of them I say, "Thank you."

Notes

[1] See encyclopedia.thefreedictionary.com/Concealed+carry+(gun+laws) Too numerous to list, the dictionaries on the web have a consistent theme which is that to conceal is to hide or secret from view with a purpose the subject matter of the concealment be "hidden." Thus the normal usage of the word "to conceal" means with the purpose of hiding or secreting.

[2] *PGE v. BOLI*, 317 Or. 606, 859 P2d 1143 (1993) According to this recent [2010] Yale Law Journal article, Oregon is not only unusual in its approach to statutory interpretation; it is "unparalleled." The mainstream academic assumption is that it's impossible to judicially create a binding precedent for statutory interpretation based on textualism. To do so without a single dissenting vote in 16 years is apparently mind boggling. Who knew? It's just our law. It's interesting to see Oregon placed into the broader sea of possibilities as well as the academic discourse. See mpdtrainer.wordpress.com/2010/08/27/pge-v-boli/

[3] PDF file at the Oregon Firearms website:
oregonfirearms.org/pdfs/Heynderickx%20Letter%20.pdf

[4] **Oregon Constitution Article IV, Section 21. Acts to be plainly worded.** Every act, and joint resolution shall be plainly worded, avoiding as far as practicable the use of technical terms.

[5] **ORS 171.134 Readability test for legislative digests and summaries.** Any measure digest or measure summary prepared by the Legislative Assembly shall be written in a manner that results in a score of at least 60 on the Flesch readability test or meets an equivalent standard of a comparable test. [1979 c.270 §1]

[6] **OAR 183.750 State agency required to prepare public writings in readable form.** (1) Every state agency shall prepare its public writings in language that is as clear and simple as possible.
(2) As used in this section:
(a) "Public writing" means any rule, form, license, or notice prepared by a state agency.
(b) "State agency" means any officer, board, commission, department, division, or institution in the executive or administrative branch of state government. [Formerly 183.025]

[7] **ORS 161.205 Use of physical force generally.** The use of physical force upon another person that would otherwise constitute an offense is justifiable and not criminal under any of the following circumstances:
(4) A person acting under a reasonable belief that another person is about to commit suicide or to inflict serious physical self-injury may use physical force upon that person to the extent that the person reasonably believes it necessary to thwart the result.

(5) A person may use physical force upon another person in self-defense or in defending a third person, in defending property, in making an arrest, or in preventing an escape, as hereafter prescribed in chapter 743, Oregon Laws 1971. [1971 c.743 §21; 1981 c.246 §1]

[8] ORS **161.209 Use of physical force in defense of a person.** Except as provided in ORS 161.215 and 161.219, a person is justified in using physical force upon another person for self-defense or to defend a third person from what the person reasonably believes to be the use or imminent use of unlawful physical force, and the person may use a degree of force which the person reasonably believes to be necessary for the purpose. [1971 c.743 §22]

[9] ORS **161.215 Limitations on use of physical force in defense of a person.** Notwithstanding ORS 161.209, a person is not justified in using physical force upon another person if:
(1) With intent to cause physical injury or death to another person, the person provokes the use of unlawful physical force by that person; or
(2) The person is the initial aggressor, except that the use of physical force upon another person under such circumstances is justifiable if the person withdraws from the encounter and effectively communicates to the other person the intent to do so, but the latter nevertheless continues or threatens to continue the use of unlawful physical force; or
(3) The physical force involved is the product of a combat by agreement not specifically authorized by law. [1971 c.743 §24]

[10] *STATE v. BASSETT*, 234 Or. App. 259 (2010), 228 P.3d 590; STATE OF OREGON, Plaintiff-Respondent, v. ANDREW LEE BASSETT, Defendant-Appellant. 080141146; A138837. Oregon Court of Appeals. Argued and submitted October 28, 2009. March 10, 2010.

[11] See web sites:
www.thefreelibrary.com/Acquitted+Dutch+Bros.+robbery+defendant+in+jail+on+new+charge.-a0266879377; www.thetruthaboutguns.com/2010/12/chris-dumm/dutch-brothers-in-arms; special.registerguard.com/csp/cms/sites/web/news/cityregion/25792735-41/combs-barista-braziel-affidavit-dutch.csp; special.registerguard.com/csp/cms/sites/web/updates/25593773-55/police-bros-dutch-shooting-coffee.csp; kezi.com/page/208355;
www.oregonlive.com/news/index.ssf/2010/11/dutch_bros_barista_shoots_kill.html

[12] I wrestle with health issues. In learning to control some of the things that impact the stressors in my life I have found and have been advised by my doctor to take "news" out of my life. Generally I do not read newspapers, watch TV news, and I do not listen to news on the radio. I do selectively research news of interest on the internet.

[13] Stephen Halbrook's *The Founders' Second Amendment* is the first book-length account of the origins of the Second Amendment, based on the Founders' own statements as found in newspapers, correspondence, debates, and resolutions. Dr. Halbrook investigates the period from 1768 to 1826, from the last years of British rule and the American Revolution through to the adoption of the Constitution and the Bill of Rights, and the passing of the Founders' generation. His book offers the most comprehensive analysis of the arguments behind the drafting and adoption of the Second Amendment, and the intentions of the men who created it.

[14] We recommend the following reading from the internet at this web site: www.constitution.org/mil/rkba1982.htm

[15] Definition of PURVIEW: www.merriam-webster.com/dictionary/purview?show=0&t=1318770339
a. the body or enacting part of a statute
b. the limit, purpose, or scope of a statute
c. the range or limit of authority, competence, responsibility, concern, or intention
d. range of vision, understanding, or cognizance. Examples follow:
1. The case is within the court's purview.
2. That question is outside my purview.
3. The moral dilemmas of the early settlers are beyond the purview of this book.

[16] "Golden years" means those years that when complied with life's experiences over time cost us a lot more gold to keep our health and what little wealth we may have managed to accumulate.

[17] **ORS 163.195**

[18] HB 2792 2011 – **SECTION 6.** ORS 821.240 is amended to read:
821.240. (1) A person commits the offense of operating a snowmobile or an all-terrain vehicle while carrying a firearm or bow if the person operates any snow-mobile or all-terrain vehicle with a firearm in the possession of the person, unless the firearm is unloaded, or with a bow, unless all arrows are in a quiver.
(2) Subsection (1) of this section does not apply to a person who is licensed under ORS 166.291 and 166.292 to carry a concealed handgun.
(3) As used in this section, "unloaded" means:
(a) If the firearm is a revolver, that there is no live cartridge in the chamber that is aligned with the hammer of the revolver;
(b) If the firearm is a muzzle-loading firearm, that the firearm is not capped or primed; or
(c) If the firearm is other than a revolver or a muzzle-loading firearm, that there is no live cartridge in the chamber.
[(2)] **(4)** The offense described in this section, operating a snowmobile or an all-terrain vehicle while carrying a firearm or bow, is a Class B traffic violation.

[19] See endnote 15 above.

[20] ORS 801.193

[21] ORS 166.250(2)(B)(b)

[22] *State v. Leslie*, 204 Or. App. 715 (2006) 132 P.3d 37; and more recently in support *Willis v. Winters*, 350 Or. 299 (2011)

[23] *State v. Honzel*, Or. App. 35 (2001).

[24] definitions.uslegal.com/c/curtilage/

[25] www.thesmokinggun.com/buster/portland/911-calls abcnews.go.com/US/home-intruder-calls-911-homeowner-caught-showering/story?id=13084609

[26] *State v. Dixson/Digby*, 307 Or. 195 (1988) 766 P.2d 1015

[27] *State v. Cardell*, 180 Or. App. 104 (2002) 41 P.3d 1111; *State v. Ohling*, 70 Or. App. 249 (1984) 688 P2.d 1384; State v. Russo, 68 Or. App. 760 (1984), 683 P.2d 163; *US v. Van Dyke*, 643 F.2d 992 (4th Cir. 1981) [FN1] The curtilage has been defined as "an area of domestic use immediately surrounding a dwelling and usually but not always fenced in with a dwelling." *United States v. LaBerger*, 267 F. Supp. 686, 692 (D.Md. 1967).

[28] ORS **161.205 Use of physical force generally.** The use of physical force upon another person that would otherwise constitute an offense is justifiable and not criminal under any of the following circumstances:
(1) A person acting under a reasonable belief that another person is about to commit suicide or to inflict serious physical self-injury may use physical force upon that person to the extent that the person reasonably believes it necessary to thwart the result.
(2) A person may use physical force upon another person in self-defense or in defending a third person, in defending property, in making an arrest or in preventing an escape, as hereafter prescribed in chapter 743, Oregon Laws 1971. [1971 c.743 §21; 1981 c.246 §1]

[29] 36 CFR Part II, Section 261.10; 43 CFR 423.10, 423.30

[30] 36 & 42 CFR "rules" passed February 22, 2010 controlling when one can carry concealed on USFS and BLM managed property.

[31] 43 CFR 20.511

[32] 49 CFR 1540.111 Carriage of weapons, explosives, incendiaries by individuals.

[33] **166.360(4) "Public building"** means a hospital, a capitol building, a public or private school, as defined in ORS 339.315, a college or university, a city hall or the residence of any state official elected by the state at large, and the grounds adjacent to each such building. The term also includes that portion of any other

building occupied by an agency of the state or a municipal corporation, as defined in ORS 297.405, other than a court facility.

339.315(3) As used in this section, "school" means:

(a) A public or private institution of learning providing instruction at levels kindergarten through grade 12, or their equivalents, or any part thereof;

(b) The grounds adjacent to the institution; and

(c) Any site or premises that at the time is being used exclusively for a student program or activity that is sponsored or sanctioned by the institution, a public school district, an education service district or a voluntary organization approved by the State Board of Education under ORS 339.430 and that is posted as such. NOTE: 339.430 involves voluntary organizations that have been approved by the State Board of Education to administer interscholastic activities.

[34] Ors 166.250(3) "Firearms carried openly in belt holsters are not concealed within the meaning of this section."

[35] ORS § 166.170 (2009) "Except as expressly authorized by state statute, the authority to regulate in any matter whatsoever the sale, acquisition, transfer, ownership, possession, storage, transportation or use of firearms or any element relating to firearms and components thereof, including ammunition, is vested solely in the Legislative Assembly."

[36] ORS § 166.370 (2009).

[37] 18 U.S.C. § 922(q) (2). Note that this law also allows an individual to have an unloaded firearm in a motor vehicle in a school-zone if it is in a locked container in the motor vehicle.

[38] The Oregon University System includes: Eastern Oregon University, Oregon Institute of Technology, Oregon State University, Portland State University, Southern Oregon University, University of Oregon, and Western Oregon University.

[39] ORS §§ 351.060, 351.070 (2009).

[40] *See* Bronson v. Moonen, 270 Or. 469, 476 (1974) "Administrative rules and regulations are to be regarded as legislative enactments having the same effect as if enacted by the legislature as part of the original statute."

[41] OAR 580-22-0045(3).

[42] *Oregon Firearms Educational Foundation v. Board of Higher Education*, No. A142974 (Or. Ct. App. September, 28 2011).

[43] ORS § 166.370 (2009).

[44] *Id.*

[45] ORS § 332.107 (2009).

⁴⁶ ORS § 332.172 (2009).

⁴⁷ *See* Bronson v. Moonen, 270 Or. 469, 476 (1974) "Administrative rules and regulations are to be regarded as legislative enactments having the same effect as if enacted by the legislature as part of the original statute."

⁴⁸ Portland Public Schools School Board Policy, 3.40.014-P.

⁴⁹ Willamette Education Service District Policy, JFCJ, Weapons in the Schools.

⁵⁰ Eugene School District 4J School Board Policy, KGB 8900, Dangerous Weapons.

⁵¹ *Id.*

⁵² *Id.*

⁵³ Springfield School District 19 Policy, JFCJ, Weapons in the Schools "Those individuals with a concealed weapons permit are asked to voluntarily comply with the intent of this policy and not bring a weapon onto district property."

⁵⁴ In a resolution passed by the Oregon School Boards Association in 2003, the OSBA stated that "Oregon law currently allows persons with concealed weapons permits to carry weapons on school property and at school-sponsored activities that are open to the public."

⁵⁵ *Doe v. Medford School Dist. 549C*, 232 Or. App. 38 (2009).

⁵⁶ ORS § 166.370 (2009).

⁵⁷ *Id.*

⁵⁸ ORS § 164.245 (2009).

⁵⁹ ORS §§ 161.615, 161.635 (2009).

⁶⁰ ORS § 164.265 (2009).

⁶¹ ORS 133.225 (1) A private person may arrest another person for any crime committed in the presence of the private person if the private person has probable cause to believe the arrested person committed the crime. A private person making such an arrest shall, without unnecessary delay, take the arrested person before a magistrate or deliver the arrested person to a peace officer.

(2) In order to make the arrest a private person may use physical force as is justifiable under ORS 161.255. [1973 c. 836 § 74] If you want to see it again, you can read it in Appendix "L".

⁶² ORS 133.225 Except as provided in subsection (2) of this section, a private person acting on the person's own account is justified in using physical force upon another person when and to the extent that the person reasonably believes it neces-

sary to make an arrest or to prevent the escape from custody of an arrested person whom the person has arrested under ORS 133.225.

(2) A private person acting under the circumstances prescribed in subsection (1) of this section is justified in using deadly physical force only when the person reasonably believes it necessary for self-defense or to defend a third person from what the person reasonably believes to be the use or imminent use of deadly physical force.

[63] See endnote 4 above for the *McDonald* case and also at en.wikipedia.org/wiki/District_of_Columbia_v._Heller which when viewed in combination with each other in substance hold that the Second Amendment of the Federal Constitution guarantees us the right to protect ourselves and to have the ability to do so by use of firearms.

[64] *BABICK v. OREGON ARENA CORP.*, 333 Or. 401 (2002), 40 P.3d 1059; KENNETH BABICK, GARY MOORE, and JACK K. MINZEY, JR., and others similarly situated, Petitioners on Review/Respondents on Review, v. OREGON ARENA CORPORATION, an Oregon Corporation, Respondent on Review/Petitioner on Review. (CC 9704-02797; CA A99542; S.C. S46518, S46578) (Consolidated for Argument and Opinion) Oregon Supreme Court. Argued and submitted September 11, 2000. **Filed:** February 22, 2002 – for the proposition of rejection of the Legislative Branch statutes as statements of the current public policy.

[65] *Willis v. Winters*, 235 Or. App 615 (2010) 234 P.3d 141; *Willis v. Winters*, 350 Or. 299 (2011)

[66] **Oregon Constitution Article 1, Section 1. Natural rights inherent in people.** We declare that all men, when they form a social compact are equal in right: that all power is inherent in the people, and all free governments are founded on their authority, and instituted for their peace, safety, and happiness; and they have at all times a right to alter, reform, or abolish the government in such manner as they may think proper. www.leg.state.or.us/orcons/orcons.html

[67] **Oregon Constitution Article 1, Section 27. Right to bear arms; military subordinate to civil power.** The people shall have the right to bear arms for the defence *[sic]* of themselves, and the State, but the Military shall be kept in strict subordination to the civil power[.]
Oregon Constitution Article 3, Section 1. Separation of powers. The powers of the Government shall be divided into three separate *[sic]* departments, the Legislative, the Executive, including the administrative, and the Judicial; and no person charged with official duties under one of these departments, shall exercise any of the functions of another, except as in this Constitution expressly provided. www.leg.state.or.us/orcons/orcons.html

[68] en.wikipedia.org/wiki/McDonald_v._Chicago *McDonald v. Chicago*, 561 U.S. ___, 130 S.Ct. 3020 (2010), was a landmark decision of the Supreme Court of the United States that determined whether the Second Amendment applies to the individual states. The Court held that the right of an individual to "keep and bear arms" protected by the Second Amendment is incorporated by the Due Process Clause of the Fourteenth Amendment and applies to the states. The decision cleared up the uncertainty left in the wake of District of Columbia v. Heller as to the scope of gun rights in regard to the states.

[69] en.wikipedia.org/wiki/District_of_Columbia_v._Heller *District of Columbia v. Heller*, 554 U.S. 570 (2008), was a landmark case in which the Supreme Court of the United States held that the Second Amendment to the United States Constitution protects an individual's right to possess a firearm for traditionally lawful purposes in federal enclaves, such as self-defense within the home. The decision did not address the question of whether the Second Amendment extends beyond federal enclaves to the states, which was addressed later by McDonald v. Chicago (2010). It was the first Supreme Court case in United States history to decide whether the Second Amendment protects an individual right to keep and bear arms for self defense. On June 26, 2008, the Supreme Court affirmed the Court of Appeals for the D.C. Circuit in *Parker v. District of Columbia*. The Court of Appeals had struck down provisions of the Firearms Control Regulations Act of 1975 as unconstitutional, determined that handguns are "arms" for the purposes of the Second Amendment, found that the District of Columbia's regulations act was an unconstitutional banning, and struck down the portion of the regulations act that requires all firearms including rifles and shotguns be kept "unloaded and disassembled or bound by a trigger lock." "Prior to this decision the Firearms Control Regulation Act of 1975 also restricted residents from owning handguns except for those registered prior to 1975."

[70] If the reader is interested in these cases, there is enough information here to do the research: *DIKA v. DIF*, 817 P.2d 287 (1991) 312 Or. 106: http://174.123.24.242/leagle/xmlResult.aspx?xmldoc=19911104817P2d287_1110 2.xml&docbase=CSLWAR2-1986-2006 *Benzinger v. DIF*; *Moonen v. Bronson*.

[71] "[The] principle [of the Constitution] is that of a separation of Legislative, Executive and Judiciary functions except in cases specified. If this principle be not expressed in direct terms, it is clearly the spirit of the Constitution, and it ought to be so commented and acted on by every friend of free government." —Thomas Jefferson to James Madison, 1797. ME 9:368
"Our Constitution has wisely distributed the administration of the government into three distinct and independent departments. To each of these it belongs to administer law within its separate jurisdiction. The Judiciary in cases of *meum* and *tuum*, and of public crimes; the Executive, as to laws executive in their nature; the Legislature in various cases which belong to itself, and in the important function of

amending and adding to the system." —Thomas Jefferson: Batture at New Orleans, 1812. ME 18:129

"The three great departments having distinct functions to perform, must have distinct rules adapted to them. Each must act under its own rules, those of no one having any obligation on either of the others." —Thomas Jefferson to James Barbour, 1812. ME 13:129

"The Constitution intended that the three great branches of the government should be co-ordinate and independent of each other. As to acts, therefore, which are to be done by either, it has given no control to another branch... Where different branches have to act in their respective lines, finally and without appeal, under any law, they may give to it different and opposite constructions... From these different constructions of the same act by different branches, less mischief arises than from giving to any one of them a control over the others." —Thomas Jefferson to George Hay, 1807. ME 11:213

[72] www.independent.org/publications/tir/article.asp?a=167 (one of many synopses) *The Tyranny of Good Intentions* should make those who participate in our political and legal systems uncomfortable, if not self-loathing. Paul Craig Roberts and Lawrence M. Stratton's principal argument is that what passes for "law" in the current civic climate is far removed from "the long struggle to establish the people's sovereignty" that dates back to pre-Norman England (p. ix). Simply put, the law has been transformed from a shield that protects the people from the encroachments of government power into a sword that enables the government to lord over the people. Those who are weary of the ongoing government assault on Microsoft and the tobacco industry or of the continued evisceration of civil liberties under the tutelary banner of the drug war should immediately recognize this transformation. Nevertheless, most Americans now tacitly assume that state power is a *source of* freedom rather than an *obstacle to* freedom.